Baby's name ....

Date of birth ....

A gift from ....

Angel Blessings
for Babies

Angel Blessings *for* Babies

AMBIKA WAUTERS

CARROLL & BROWN PUBLISHERS LIMITED

First published in 2010 in the United Kingdom by

Carroll & Brown Publishers Limited
20 Lonsdale Road
Queen's Park
London NW6 6RD

A CIP catalogue record for this book is available from
The British Library.

ISBN 978-1-904760-82-5

10 9 8 7 6 5 4 3 2 1

Reproduced by Rali, Spain
Printed and bound in China

CONTENTS

INTRODUCTION

 *Angel Blessings for Babies* is a book for all those welcoming a new baby into the world. It incorporates the rich and bountiful blessings of the angelic realm for new life and provides angelic guidance, meditations and prayers that can touch the lives and spirits of families, both immediate and extended, and all who come into contact with babies.

The book offers spiritual support, enabling readers to connect with the purity and goodness that babies bring into the world. Readers should be able to form a deep, enriching bond with a baby, which will be sustained by unconditional love and absolute and total acceptance. This foundation ensures a baby's internal stability, sense of wholeness and unity with all life – qualities that are intrinsic to the spiritual makeup needed to live in the world and fulfill one's life's calling.

For parents, the book offers spiritual guidance for accepting the demanding tasks they face in a loving way. It should help them to embrace the core values of love, acceptance and unconditional, unqualified care.

The book also acknowledges the vital role of parents in guiding young spirits into life. By working with the prayers and meditations the book contains, parents have the opportunity to release old childhood wounds which, if left unresolved, may limit the full expression of their love and joy for their baby. A baby's future happiness depends on the healthy, life-sustaining bonds that are rooted in love and devotion, which mother, father and baby share. If a family has a spiritual life and is receptive to the love and guidance of the angelic realm, all members will feel at ease requesting angelic assistance.

The impulse to petition the angels for help is deeply ingrained. It is fundamental to our human development and is acknowledged by all religions. Angels freely provide help to all who want to open their hearts and expand their love. No one need struggle alone when he or she embraces angelic guidance.

Ambika Wauters

ARIES BABIES

Aries babies display a variety of temperaments equivalent to sunshine, clouds and rain – all within minutes of one another. In short order, they can be tough and gentle, irritable and loving, confident and in need of praise.

Generally, Aries are idealists who will fight for injustice and champion the underdog. They are not afraid of failure and will put their hearts and souls into something; if they fall down, they will pick themselves up and try again. They are very direct in their demeanours and will go straight to the point. With Aries, what you see is who

they are. There is nothing hidden, complicated or cunning. We recognise the Aries adult by her forceful presence, her firm and inviting handshake and that instant smile that is so delightful and engaging.

However, Aries are self-absorbed and their needs will always be expressed first; they relate to the world as it relates to them. When an Aries is opposed, loud screams follow. People often give them just what they want simply to keep them quiet. Therefore, an Aries baby will let you know in no uncertain terms what irritates or bothers her.

Aries babies need clear discipline as they can be very defiant and not easy to control. Feeding an Aries baby can be a challenge as she will put the bowl of cereal on her head and spit out those vegetables you think might be good for her. Parenting can be quite a challenge; you need to find the middle ground where you are loving and encouraging and full of praise, when appropriate, but also able to set boundaries and be willing to enforce them.

Aries babies walk and talk early and you'll need to guard against falls and injuries to your baby's head. Like the ram, which is the symbol for Aries, these children will butt heads with reality often

ANGELIC GUIDANCE

Please help me to parent my Aries baby with constancy and strength. Help me bring out what is loving, creative and genuine in my child without being intimidated by her temper or willfulness. I know this child has gifts and I wish to respect them and create wholesome boundaries that help my baby to find balance and order in the world.

in their lives. They can, for example, have a challenging time teething.

Aries babies are affectionate and demonstrative and love strong bear hugs. They respond beautifully to praise. They can be generous until their feelings are hurt and then they will show signs of temper.

They make very good students and have vivid imaginations – particularly enjoying stories of conquering heroes – but dislike surprises or anything that will disrupt their fragile confidence. They become leaders in their own unique ways. They have a deep-seated fear of being disliked and not being loved. Despite their brave fronts they are sensitive idealists who bruise easily; they do not like to be unkind or cruel.

Dearest Angel of Aries Babies, *please help my baby grow into a loving and responsible person who can feel the needs of others and give heartfelt love to those who care for her needs. Help us to create a deep sense of truth, love and goodness in our child and support every effort we make to bring a fine person into the world.*

9

THE HOLY ORIGINS OF LIFE

This beautiful painting is meant to show us that the heavens upheld the coming of the Christ incarnated into a human body. The angels in heaven, which surround the Madonna and child, applaud His presence. All life comes from spirit and all babies remind us that our origins are holy, spiritual and sacred to the realm of angels and to the Creator.

Angels are known as God's messengers. They carry the highest impulse for good, along with unconditional love for who we are and how we live our lives. They support us with wisdom, guidance, right action and a deepening sense of our wholeness. They are our friends, our cherished companions along the path of life. They have been a part of our souls' developments since the beginning of humanity and will remain with us through eternity.

As we develop into spiritual beings, conscious of truth, love and kindness, they work more fully on our behalf to support the flow of love and harmony in our lives. We call on them for help, protection and guidance when we do not have answers to the challenges facing us. Our angels are always attentive to our needs; they need

only to be asked for their help. Just as each person has his or her guardian angel, each stage of life is supported by angels as well. There are, for example, angels for mothers and fathers, sisters and brothers, aunts and uncles, grandparents and godparents. It says in the Talmud that there is an angel for every blade of grass. As you step into your destiny as a parent or close family member, you can be assured that your baby also has her angel, helping her to come into life in a good and loving way.

This chapter offers the love and guidance of the Angel of the Holy Origins of Life, that precious recognition that life originates not in matter but in spirit, which is made flesh. It enables the love of the Angel of Acceptance, that place deep within ourselves where we make our lives and where we are right for ourselves; and finally, the Angel of Parents To Be, the great source of love and guidance for those who are about to take on the mantle of parenting.

Our destiny is to know who we are and where we come from, which way to go beyond the material plane and earthly existence. If we believe that life is only material and mechanical, we miss much of

PART

1

the truth of our origins. First and foremost, we are spiritual beings. Our origins are in the spiritual realm and are determined by the unshakable laws of the universe. We come to earth to fulfill the divine intentions of love, truth and consciousness.

When we acknowledge our spiritual origins, we affirm our connection with the angels and the entire spiritual hierarchy. We bring to consciousness, in a living way, the love of God for all humanity. When we cultivate a spiritual context for grasping life's realities, we grow in spirit and are better able to accommodate the challenges life brings us. We open doors to the truth of love, joy, healing and wholeness.

What we chose to do with our lives will either expand or diminish the reality of our spiritual origins. Staying connected with the Source, which is the living presence of God within us, is a wonderful way of living a conscious life. We build our moral impulses and allow them to work in us, as us and through us in our hearts and minds. This is the greatest heritage we can pass on to our children.

In Raphael's picture, The Foligno Madonna, *the Madonna tickles her baby and he is content and at ease in his mother's arms. This is a simple human act of mother and child united together in love, joy and delight in the presence of various saints and the painting's donor.*

THE ANGEL OF The Holy Origins of Life

"I affirm the holy origins
of my life.
I know my life and
the life of my child has
a spiritual purpose"

ANGELIC GUIDANCE

I ask for a deeper understanding of the holy origins of life. I seek help in accepting that my baby has chosen me for his parent and our home in which to grow and thrive. I acknowledge the choices I make now for love, happiness and wholeness. Help me acknowledge my baby's choices as well. I know my new baby will bring God's love to heal us all. I know he will have his own life and destiny. Help me to accept and listen for angelic guidance in making wise and wholesome choices for my baby.

The holy origins of life are an essential part of our beginning on Earth; they are the very bedrock of our being. Yet it is easy to forget that we are spiritual beings and that our origins (as do all creatures), lie in the spiritual realm because too often we identify with the cultural maze in which we live, the exterior reality of the physical and material world.

Before life takes on physical form, it exists in the realm of creation called the spiritual world. Within this realm, the angels guide our souls' paths and help them become pure vessels for life. Angels ensure that God's unconditional love carries us into life and that we experience the truth that we are loved, cherished and protected by our angelic guides at all times.

The Angel of the Holy Origins of Life reminds us that we choose our lives – family, cultural circumstances and physical condition – and that these choices are part of our destiny. We have all incarnated to help humanity in one form or another in its struggle to develop. We each play a part in humanity's continual evolution towards a higher good, in which we love one another, and heal and make whole our planet. The spiritual challenges we will face in this life will ultimately fortify our souls' capacities to love, develop self- expression and experience wholeness.

The angels affirm our wholeness. They encourage us to grow and develop into worthy beings who can experience and give love and who are able to hold the space for good to unfold. We are each given the right circumstances to develop ourselves as earth angels; God's children who can benefit humanity.

We each choose the parents who will mould and influence our characters and who will provide the right environment for our soul's growth. We call in the siblings who will be a part of our understanding of other people and how they function and think.

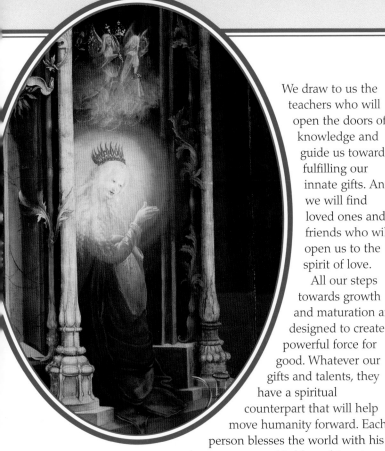

We draw to us the teachers who will open the doors of knowledge and guide us towards fulfilling our innate gifts. And we will find loved ones and friends who will open us to the spirit of love.

All our steps towards growth and maturation are designed to create a powerful force for good. Whatever our gifts and talents, they have a spiritual counterpart that will help move humanity forward. Each person blesses the world with his or her presence and is blessed in return by the spiritual world as a significant contributor to the lessons humanity will embody as it becomes more spiritually aware.

Angels believe in us. They communicate to us that all is well. Their hope is that we learn to love and accept ourselves fully so we can be greater channels for love. Angels help nurture the gifts we bring into the world; they help us expand our consciousness. At a personal level, they offer each of us healing for the wounds life brings and, at a collective level, they heal the earth.

Angelic Prayer
....

Dearest Angel of the Holy Origins of Life, please open the window of consciousness in my mind so I may see the Divine within myself and my new baby. May this understanding bring us closer to the experience of God's love and inspire us to reach out to His angels for the help we need in life. Please help us share our love in ways that heal the world around us.

 ## Meditation

As I sit in peace and quiet, visualising my baby alive within me, I reflect on the holy origins of my own life. I accept God's wish that the Divine be revealed through each individual as I honour His gift of life to me. My angel awaits my awakening to the truth that I know my life is holy and that my child is holy. I affirm my worth in every way and I honour my life. I acknowledge the challenges that afford me growth and help me to appreciate happiness and joy as they flow into my life right now.

THE ANGEL OF Acceptance

"I accept and love myself exactly as I am. In loving myself I accept my child exactly as he will be. Acceptance is honouring the incontrovertible truth that life is a great gift"

ANGELIC GUIDANCE

I seek to look within to prepare myself to be a parent and to know what path will be best for my baby. Please guide me to the full experience of my own wholeness, so I don't impose my desires for fulfillment onto my child. I know when I accept myself as a divine creature of God then I will fully accept my baby as the same. Please guide me in doing this consciously and with grace.

Being spiritually prepared for a new baby helps parents accept and graciously welcome a baby into life. The experience of parenthood may not be new but it is always unique. Each child has his own special essence, which parents must learn to understand and accept. Accepting a new baby exactly as he is will be nurturing and healing to his soul, and allows him the space to fulfill his destiny. To know that your child has his own separate, individual life is also liberating for you as a parent; you can rejoice in being a guide to your child as his gifts develop without being burdened with thinking you must create a perfect human being.

Babies choose families that are best matched to the development of their individual gifts. Even a difficult family situation will mould the spirit of a child and help him grow and develop strengths that will be useful in later life. The Angel of Acceptance will guide each and every person to find his or her way to healing and offers help in challenging circumstances.

As a parent, you can consciously support your baby's development through abiding love and unconditional acceptance. The more you love and accept yourself, the easier it is for you to embrace your child fully. When you accept that you are loved, you will make better choices for yourself and your family. When you accept yourself, you give your child the space to accept who he is and to come closer to defining the purpose of his life.

Babies always teach us about love. That is their mission statement as they enter life. Wise parents accept this and love and accept their children as gifts.

When you are prepared to provide your baby with the foundation of a loving environment and clean and attractive surroundings in which his spirit can flourish, you allow him to develop in a stream of light and goodness.

Angelic Prayer

· · · · · · · · · · · · · · · · · ·

*Dearest Angel of Acceptance, please guide
me to love and accept my new baby exactly
as he is. I pray to love and accept even
what I cannot understand. I know my
child has his own destiny to fulfill in his
generation, in his culture and by himself.
Help me accept my baby as the perfect
expression of God's love and to cultivate
true acceptance of myself so that I may
enjoy, love and nurture us both.*

 ## Meditation

*I open my body as a vessel for the physical
form of the loving spirit that grows and
develops within. I open my heart to the
loving spirit, which will help me be a good
parent, both loving and fulfilling my
baby's needs. I open my mind to knowing
that it is only through acceptance that
I truly support this beautiful being and
enable him to be his best. I allow myself to
receive my good and to be fully prepared
spiritually for the role of parenthood.
I accept my self; I accept the changes that
are happening to me; I accept life!*

When babies are truly accepted, they experience safety and love.
Acceptance helps them release any unconscious fears they may
have brought into this life. Doubt or fear only makes babies
contract their spirits as a way to survive.

When babies are able to express their unique natures freely,
their life paths can easily unfold over time. Highly ambitious
parents, who have big plans for their children, however,
sometimes force their babies to sacrifice their innate, God-given
gifts to accommodate the parents' wishes. While babies will make
this sacrifice out of love for their parents, great gifts that may be
given to the world may be hidden by conventional thinking or by
parents' wishes that their children follow in their footsteps.

TAURUS BABIES

Taureans are delightful as babies and children. They love affection and are cuddly and loving and enjoy the warmth of your touch. They can be sweet and even flirtatious. Generally cheerful, they are predictable and good in front of strangers as long as you leave them to play and not make them the centre of attention.

Taureans respond well to common sense, simplicity and truth. Competent even as toddlers, they show signs of emotional stability and are not easily disturbed or subject to mood shifts. They are capable of lasting love and are loyal to their families and friends.

They do not like to show off and can be shy, timid and stubborn. They like to be left alone and do not respond to being pushed or forced to do what they do not want to do. Consequently, they can be challenging to dress, feed and bathe. Always speak gently and logically to your Taurus baby. If you are too harsh, he will withdraw and resist you. Taureans are never rude or nasty but cannot stand to be teased. A big hug and kiss can coax them out of their bad moods.

Taurus children love to paint and draw and are able to express their natures through art. They are industrious students and learn easily if they are taught to be methodical in their application. They have a good ability to concentrate, are obedient and, though they absorb slowly, have wonderful retentive memories and a large capacity for work and responsibility.

They move deliberately and speak little. They are solid and steady even predictable, and little disturbs their innate tranquillity. Simple and uncomplicated, they are not given to subtlety or worrying; they let life bring things to them rather than going in hot pursuit of others or objects of desire. They can be slow at making decisions but fast at calculating results.

ANGELIC GUIDANCE

Please help me teach my Taurus baby to adapt to the rhythms and cycles of life. I know that his nature is strong and tied to the earth and that he will thrive when he is in synchronicity with the day and night and the seasons. Help me open his heart to feeling safe and loved.

April 21st - May 20th

Taureans are homebodies and enjoy security. They love creature comforts and can be possessive about their belongings. They love good food and drink, good art and music and the best of everything.

They can bear up under emotional stress and not complain or be upset by crisis. It is said of Taurus that the greater the trouble, the more strength he produces to overcome it. Hearty and healthy with strong constitutions, it takes a lot to make Taureans ill, but once in bed, they are slow to recuperate. They can be stubborn and do not like to follow the doctor's orders.

Taureans can be conservative with their finances. They like to build and can create an empire slowly and deliberately. They enjoy accumulating power and money and have a strong potential for amassing wealth.

* * *

Dearest Angel of Taurus Babies, *please help me encourage my child to try and adapt to new things, new foods, new people. I know that his nature is stubborn and fixed. I pray that my baby responds with a sense of safety to life and to those who have his best interests at heart. Help me inspire him to take risks and enjoy adventures.*

17

THE ANGEL OF Parents To Be

"I have all that I need within me to be a wonderful, loving parent to my baby"

Babies are gifts from God and bring love, beauty and peace to the world. They are the hope for a better life and carry the potential to do good and heal the world; they are the future of humanity. Babies carry the sweetness and perfection of the spiritual world. The angels are close to babies in the softness of their skins and the sweet smell of their breaths. Babies hold us captive with their smiles, peeps or coos, and especially their cries. We listen, attend to their wishes and resonate in the joy and wonder they bring us.

Becoming a parent is a milestone of adult maturity and comes with immense responsibilities. Babies require loving attention in order to thrive, and constant vigilance to ensure their safety and protection. Their newly developing and delicate nervous systems require tenderness and care after their long journeys from the angelic realm into the world of form and matter. And in order for your baby to become the adult you wish him to be – capable and responsible, able to make choices and wise decisions – you need to be his role model. These can be daunting tasks, especially for first-time parents.

This is where the Angel of Parents To Be can be a wonderful guide. It can help you tune into your baby and support a healthy parent-baby relationship that enables you to be in harmony with one another. It can encourage good parenting skills and give you guidance indoing what baby needs to thrive and be healthy.

For some people it may be an effortless task to step into the role of provider and caregiver. For others, those who are challenged by parental responsibilities, it may be important to know there is help in the form of the beloved angels who provide help for whatever your needs may be. Angels can make parenting flow with ease and lend a sense of grace to the tasks at hand.

ANGELIC GUIDANCE

I seek support for my family and myself in welcoming new life. Help us to find merit in our efforts and to be aware of the huge task we face. Support us in nurturing our baby so he feels safe in the world. Help our families and friends understand the job we have before us and let them support our efforts to the best of their abilities. Bless me as a new parent and encourage me to persevere through the ups and downs of parenting and the challenges life will inevitably bring me.

Angelic Prayer

Dearest Angel of Parents To Be, I pray to you to support me and my family in caring for and loving our new baby. May our joy see us through the demands of parenting. Help us to stay close as a family and look after our needs as well as those of our child.

 ## Meditation

I sit in silence and listen to the voices of angels whispering in my ears the truth of who this baby will be in my life. I seek to be given truths about the beauty, peace and wholeness possible to us both as I rest in the peace of the angels' love. Angels are there to encourage me to be the best parent possible. They honour me, my family and my child with their love, wisdom and joy as I take on the mantle of parenting. I know the angels bless me and offer me their full help in parenting.

RADIANT EXPECTANCY

As you come to accept the role of motherhood and embrace the changes pregnancy brings, you become radiant and beautiful. Your body will become softer, more rounded and will glow with life. You become the quintessential embodiment of the divine symbol for life – a mother.

If you willingly embrace motherhood, you open yourself to the deepest truths about life and love. These truths add to the richness of your beauty and give you a quality of wisdom. Your priorities about life shift from the external and material world to a deep, internal awareness that you are close to the divine source of life.

If you wish to engage with angels, they will whisper in your ears, be your guide and pilot you through the long months of gestation. You have the opportunity to know many spiritual truths during this time before giving birth. If you call on your angels, they will assuage your fears and soothe your spirit. They will help you experience the child within you. You can begin to know your baby's nature even before she is born. You can communicate with her, and assure her she is welcome and wanted. Angels support this growing connection between you and your baby during pregnancy.

Pregnancy is a time of new beginnings, where love is abundant and flowing. No matter how our lives develop, there is always the core memory of love. If, in anxieties about forthcoming parenthood, you forget the truth of your beginning, you can ask to be connected to the source of love through The Angel of Expectant Radiance. This angel enables you to remember whom you are, that you were once deeply loved and nurtured and that you can bestow these gifts on your child.

Being pregnant, you carry the forces of life within you. You are the crucible from which life emerges and are, therefore, sacred and blessed by the Angel of Growth and Healing. You can also call on The Angel of Blessed Delivery to help you feel secure in the birthing process. Invoking this help before birth will enable you to feel confident, courageous and resilient during birth. The Angel of Post Partum Healing helps facilitate a fast and speedy recovery from birth and enables sufficient milk for you to nurse. The angelic realm awaits your request for help.

PART

2

In Raphael's picture, The Seggiola Madonna, *the Madonna and Christ child appear slightly hesitant about stepping out into the world. Both their expressions show a timidity and a reticence about coming forward. The world, however, awaits this child's coming with hopes for redemption. All children are sent into the world in hopes they will bring redemption for suffering and make a better world. Each generation carries that mantle and brings us closer in spiritual evolution to a clearer awareness of our spiritual purpose and how we can heal the world.*

THE ANGEL OF
Expectant Radiance

*"I am radiant and beautiful
as I accept the blessings of
impending motherhood"*

ANGELIC GUIDANCE

As my body changes, help me calm my
spirit and respond to its needs for peace,
tranquillity and positive thoughts. I seek
guidance for the duration of my
pregnancy for what is good and nurturing
for me and my baby. I ask for the rest my
spirit longs for and the stimulation of
appropriate exercise, if that should be
necessary for our wellbeing.

When you are pregnant, the miracle of
life taking place within the universe of
your body causes it to emanate radiance
and joy. As you experience the origins
of life, every cell in your body is
stimulated to expand with a vibrancy
uncommon in ordinary life. You are a
woman blessed.

As your baby grows and your body
expands to contain her, a deep inner
knowing takes hold and expresses itself
in practical wisdom, secret occult
knowledge and a grasp of universal
truths. You become radiant in
knowledge and in the expression of life
moving in and through you.

This flush of life captivates others
because it touches the core of their
being, reminding them that life is
sacred. If the truth of your beginning is
forgotten, however, you can always ask
to be connected to the source of love
through the Angel of Expectant
Radiance. This angel allows you to
remember who you are and that you
were once deeply loved and nurtured.
No matter how your life develops, there
is always the core memory of love.

Angelic Prayer

Dearest Angel of Expectant Radiance, I pray to you to help me understand the changes taking place in my body, mind and spirit. Help me honour my needs for nurturing myself, so I can get plenty of rest, proper nutrition and whatever else I need for my baby to thrive within me and grow into a healthy and happy being. I give thanks for the miracle of life.

 ## Meditation

Experience the silence within yourself. Ask yourself "What do I need to support my happiness and wellbeing right now? The answer may be rest, movement, or perhaps ceasing to worry about small things. Whatever the answer, acknowledge your connection to your angels as real and happening now. The more you seek guidance, the easier and more tranquil this pregnancy will be for you and baby. The angels support you and your baby.

THE ANGEL OF Growth and Healing

*"As my baby grows within
I forgive and release any pain
from my past"*

ANGELIC GUIDANCE

I seek to release the hurts of the past and affirm the joy of life within me. Help me listen internally to my baby, and to accept the deeply peaceful part of my own nature that abides in this silence. I hope to reflect on what the angels whisper in my ears. It may be baby's name, for example, or what colour to paint her room, or what special toys to get. I treasure the guidance I will receive and I will be grateful to the angels for sharing their knowing with me. As I tune into my inner world, my focus becomes clear, cheerful and happy. This is a unique and beautiful time for which I will always be grateful.

As your pregnancy develops and your baby grows, you may find yourself seeking inner knowing that all is well, that your baby is fine, and that life is good. This is an important time for your spiritual growth. It is also a time to enjoy the pleasures of life. You have the opportunity to resonate with the cycles of the natural world and to experience that you and your baby are united to all life.

During pregnancy, your baby's spirit is strongly connected to the angelic world although her physical body is becoming rooted in the world of substance and matter. The meeting of heaven and earth takes place in your baby. As you walk, swim, do yoga, sing, laugh or cry (if need be), being moved and touched by the absolute miracle of life will help your baby's spirit chose this physical life and incarnate into her body. Your happiness supports her growth and development in every way.

Stay conscious as your body changes. Purify your mind by honouring your own spirit's need for rest, joy and contentment. You cleanse your spirit as life unfolds within you for the simple reason that carrying any negativity in this precious time weights your spirit down. You want to be light in spirit yet deeply connected to the cosmic forces that govern the laws of life, and which flow through your being during pregnancy. These make you more vulnerable and emotional.

This is a time to respect and respond to the internal processes that allow you to soften, release the hurts of the past, and unite yourself in the spirit of love with the great forces of life.

Angelic Prayer

*Dearest Angel of Growth and Healing,
I pray to you to support my baby in her
growth and development. Let life move in
and through me and help me prepare my
mind and body for the efforts of birthing.
Teach me the eternal truths of love and life
so that I can hold my baby in the deepest
light of universal bliss. I ask that this
pregnancy be stable, happy and easy.*

 ## Meditation

*Whenever you can, sit quietly and tune into
yourself. As you relax, focus on your
breathing and feel life moving through you.
Feel your baby, listen to her speak to you.
These moments of quiet introspection are
good for you both and help you to know
each other. You can tap into your baby's
rhythms and cycles of the day and know
when she rests and when she is active. Keep
cultivating this relationship of love and
understanding. Celebrate your miracle of
life in gratitude and joy. Surrender to the
power of life surging through you.*

GEMINI BABIES

Gemini babies are bright, busy, active, energetic, impatient, enthusiastic, eager and always on the go. They have very mercurial natures and talk and walk – quickly – at an early age. As they mature, they are good at thinking on their feet. They have sharp, clever minds and make good speakers and writers. They are satirical and clever, and, even when quite young, good mimics but the Gemini child can scream loudly and often.

Geminis love multitasking; they suffer with monotony and drudgery.

They adore change and adapt well to new experiences. They are, however, reluctant to be pinned down to an opinion and are famous for changing their minds.

Your Gemini baby needs plenty of rest to soothe his active mind and body. Rest renews his over-active brain cells and jangled nerves. It is best to slow your quicksilver child down for his own good. A Gemini can suffer from nervous exhaustion from being endlessly active so it is important to monitor your baby's activities to make sure he does not become hyper-active with too much play and not enough down time. He may, however, be a restless sleeper so the less stimulation he has at night before bed the better. Be aware of what he watches on television and listens to at bedtime and with whom he plays with in the evening. You'll want to start preparing your baby for bed as the sun goes down to ensure he gets a good night's sleep and sufficient rest.

Geminis can be demanding children. They can be everywhere at once and do not do well confined to tight, small spaces; they need room to move around. They can be fidgety and restless unless given proper stimulation; you need to offer your child a variety of toys and books.

ANGELIC GUIDANCE

Please give me the ability to keep up with my child and not be worn down by his quickness and alertness. I hope to encourage my child to be creative, expressive and inquisitive. I ask for help in differentiating when my child needs help and when it is best to allow him to discover truth for himself. Help me be consistent, resourceful and diligent in setting and keeping healthy boundaries.

May 21st - June 21st

Gemini children are good in school and wonderful communicators; they are often very good linguists, able to speak and learn several languages quickly. They have good imaginations and love to play fantasy games and engage in dress-up scenarios. Friendly, inquisitive and precocious, they also have a tendency to exaggerate and can be prone to half truths. Keep a close watch on how your child feeds back his experience of reality to you and help him to clarify reality from fiction without injuring that precious imagination.

Follow through can be a Gemini's weak point so it is good to encourage your child to complete the creative projects he starts.

Dearest Angel of Gemini Babies, *I pray for the resiliency and capacity to meet my child at each level of mind, spirit and body. I know this active child wants and needs proper stimulation and a strong moral fibre to always be in truth with himself and the world around him. Help us all to find a harmonious balance that includes love, affection, rationality and purpose.*

THE ANGEL OF Blessed Delivery

All mothers pray for a safe and swift delivery. Prayers support the process of birth to unfold in a good way. You can pray that you have the resiliency and stamina required, the right attitude of surrender and the heart to love it all.

While modern medicine has helped safeguard mothers and babies from many dangers related to birth, it has diminished the spiritual aspects of birthing that make birth a celebration of life. But prayer and invocation are powerful tools to help both mother and baby.

You can talk to your angels and ask for a safe and beautiful birthing experience. You can consciously release your fears by naming them and assuring yourself you will be fine, that your baby is beautiful and all will be well. You should do all that you can to prepare yourself for a good experience and offer your prayers for an easy and safe delivery and right action on the part of all involved in bringing your baby into the world.

In the months leading up to your delivery, talk calmly and tenderly to your baby each day. Tell her you long to hold and love her. Encourage her to arrive easily and without drama. When your baby knows you are confident and ready to welcome her, she will find her way into your arms easily and readily. You set the tone for the good to unfold for you both.

It is best to understand that each child comes into the world in her own time, with her own rhythm and at her own pace. Let your baby know she is welcomed in every way and that her rhythm will be honoured. When these truths that offer baby a safe place have been communicated, labour can begin and, unsurprisingly, birth can be swift and efficient. Communicating with your baby and your angels helps facilitate the process in a joyful and glorious way.

ANGELIC GUIDANCE

Help is needed to open my mind to positive attitudes of the birthing experience. Allow me to tune into my body so I may give birth in a conscious and positive way. Help me listen to what my baby needs in order for her to come into the world with ease and joy. She may need greater peace and freedom from strife and harmony to feel safe in arriving. Help me to honour her needs through affirming our wellbeing. Guide me to know that I approach birth with positive thoughts and loving prayers.

Angelic Prayer

....

*Dearest Angel of Blessed Delivery, I pray
to deliver my child in a safe and efficient
manner. Let the occasion be joyful and
happy. I pray for the goodness and
kindness of people who will share in my
experience and members of my family who
hold me in love. I pray for my baby to
come safely into the world. I welcome my
baby and ask your help.*

 ## Meditation

*Visualise yourself holding your baby in
your arms and feeling the flow of love
embrace you both. Be creative as you
conjure up helpful surroundings and an
easy, uncomplicated delivery. See yourself
holding your baby, who is smiling, healthy
and radiant. The more joyful and
harmonious the experience you visualise,
the more it will manifest in reality. You
can make your baby's entry into the world
beautiful, loving and joyful. Remember to
say, "Thank you" for the gift of birth. The
angels will sing and the Creator smile as
your baby begins her life.*

29

THE ANGEL OF Post Partum Healing

"I love and thank my body for the good work in did in birthing my baby. I treat it with love and care and allow it to heal and regain its form, tone and energy"

After baby's delivery, you face several challenges. In order for your body to heal, regain its tone and produce adequate milk, you require rest and proper nutrition. You also need to recoup your mental capacities so that you can deal with the many new demands – including warmth, love and nurturing – made on you by your infant. As a new mother, however, the hormonal changes that occur can make you feel vulnerable and bring unresolved emotions to the surface.

There is no better time to ask the angels for help. They support new mothers in getting their tasks accomplished and can be of great assistance when it comes to caring for babies. Call on them for help with your needs. They are always there to lighten your load and bring happiness and healing to you and your baby.

This is a time for you to re-define yourself on many levels. You need to adjust to your baby's cycles of waking and sleeping. When your baby sleeps, you sleep; when your baby wakes, give full attention to meeting her needs. Your baby will be grateful for your care and attention when she is awake and for peace when she is sleeping. You need to take advantage of her quiet times to nap, bathe, attend to other family members or simply relax. Be patient in the process of healing. It can take up to one year to regain your levels of energy and focus after baby arrives.

30

Angelic Prayer

Dearest Angel of Post Partum Healing,
please accept my gratitude for the birth of
this new child in my life. Please help me
with the simple and small chores that need
to be done to help my baby thrive in my
care. Please protect us. Show me ways
I can take care of myself, heal my body and
be a wonderful mother to my child.
I am grateful for your help.

 ## Meditation

Reflect on what you need to make yourself
feel good and to enjoy these early days of
your baby's life. Make this simple for
yourself by listing what would help you.
Perhaps someone doing the laundry for a
few days or shopping for food or even
preparing it. You may need a massage or
more bedrest to heal your body. Can you
allow yourself to ask for help so that you
can get what you need? Let joy and ease
find their way into your life in every act of
tending to your own and your child's
needs. Know in your heart that you
deserve this help and are blessed.

31

BONDING WITH BABY

Bonding is the intimate connection that takes place between mother and baby in the first days of life. Through it, a baby awakens to the warmth, love and tenderness that life can offer, and a mother is helped to establish an indestructible link of love that will connect her and her child for a lifetime.

You will have other love relationships in your life but none with the potency of this first bond uniting baby and mother, spirit and flesh, heaven and earth. Within it are the seeds of all future relationships. It explains how you connect with the world, see your place in it and fulfill your destiny. If you did not feel loved or welcomed into life, your later connections may seem very challenging. But if you felt loved, welcomed and warmed by your mother's love, then whatever life throws at you will be manageable because of the profound truth that first experience of love gives you.

Take time to develop your relationship with your baby. Bonding is not something you thrust on a baby but it develops with constancy, affirmative touch and true love. Whatever your baby brings with him from the spirit realm and past incarnations will

be expressed in how he latches on to your breast, delights in your touch and responds to your voice.

Angels offer you their love and guidance in bonding with your baby. They know that the purest archetypes of love begin with mother and child. They can help you form that union that nothing can tear apart – not even death. You can ask the angels to offer you their help. They will do all in their power to form the ties of love that create safety and trust between you and your baby.

The Angel of Bonding helps you know you are equal to the task; the Angel of Tenderness lets you experience and express the love you feel for your baby; the Angel of Simplicity reveals how simply bonding can be managed; the Angel of Tranquillity encourages you to embrace peace and its gifts and the Angel of Ease helps you allow your good to find you.

You can assist the bonding process by being careful with what you eat so as to keep your milk sweet tasting. You can use natural remedies to relieve birth trauma and help your body mend easily. Simple massage strokes can relax your baby's tight muscles after months of being confined. In

some cultures, mothers and babies are massaged for a prolonged time. Give some attention to investigating techniques, which can make it easier for your baby to want to be a part of life and close to you. Even if bonding takes several weeks to establish, don't take it personally if your baby is not yet ready to "be here". You will eventually make a relationship that resonates with love, truth and beauty. These qualities are what a baby brings to life from the spirit world. It is his gift to us all.

Raphael's Granduca Madonna *shows us love and tenderness and a bond so rich and deep that mother and child seem enveloped in one another. The Madonna gently supports her baby tenderly and gently and he holds onto her. They are united, lovingly intertwined, calm and tranquil. They are at ease one with one another – no friction, no pulling away. The baby is contemplative and the mother reflective, even slightly sad. She is deeply connected from her heart to her baby's heart, where his hand rests on her chest. They are a unit. Baby is completely bonded, safe in his mother's arms, eyes open, aware and looking out on the world.*

THE ANGEL OF Bonding

"I bond with my baby

in pure love and joy".

Bonding between mother and baby usually happens in the early days of life. It requires patience, a sense of profound purpose and love to make a baby feel he belongs and is welcome. You and your baby are energetically one being. Your baby is so completely dependent on your love, nurturing and care that he forces you to be present and available. The more you love your baby, the stronger the bond will be between you. The best that can happen is that you begin to fall in love with your baby and are consumed with his health and welfare. All your attention needs to be focused on your baby.

If you feel anxious or fearful, your baby will begin to withdraw. He will not feel the safety and warmth that welcomes him to share in love. He needs assurance that all is well. The only person who can really give this is you.

You need to know that you are adequate to the tasks of meeting your baby's needs, which will ensure his health and welfare. A baby requires warmth, food and to be free of fear. He desires only to be fed and held close to his mother. You need to know that you can produce sufficient milk, be capable and have the right attitude in tending to your baby's needs. You are the anchor your baby has to life. He only asks you to be present and approach him with love.

Bonding is sweet, tender and easy; it takes only a willingness to serve the needs of your baby and to see that all is well with him.

Angelic Prayer

Dearest Angel of Bonding, help me form a life-long link with my baby. I pray for a healthy and loving relationship as he grows into maturity and takes his place in the world. Help me heal any wounds of separation, which limit my experience of love. Help me be open to love and available for him. I want our relationship to endure and withstand the challenges life brings our way.

 ## Meditation

Know in your heart you are complete, whole and adequate in every way and fully able to provide love, care and nurturing for your baby right now. Feel the love and trust your baby gives to you. Enjoy getting to know one another. Breathe deeply and, as you breathe, take in love, let out love, take in life, let out life. As you open your heart, you will receive baby's love for you right back. This will hold you and sustain you as you look after him.

THE ANGEL OF Tenderness

"Tenderness opens my heart
and allows love to flow
between me and my baby"

Tenderness enables you to express the love and joy you feel for your new baby. It lets you experience the depths of love that live deep in your heart. Being tender with your baby opens the floodgates of tenderness that lie within, and once opened, it is impossible to stop the flow. Tenderness becomes a natural part of your being. The great Angel of Tenderness carries your love to your baby and then out to the world.

Tenderness is one of the major blessings of parenting. It is nature's way of enabling you to convey the love of God and His angels through your gentle touch, loving gaze and the sweetness of your voice. It teaches you that you are a beautiful, radiant, spiritual being and that your child will adore every look, touch, embrace and word that comes from you. In being tender and loving, your baby will easily learn what is pleasant. Your tenderness becomes a marker for what is good and what makes your child happy. The tender expression of your love will help your baby grow into a wholesome and resilient child and, later on, a balanced adult.

It is easy to love your new bundle of joy and beauty and to be tender, soft and caring to him. Show your baby your warm and vulnerable side and allow your love to flow from your heart to his. If you stay anchored in love, the daily chores of taking care of him will never become mechanical. They will reflect your sweet nature and your tender bonds ensuring that your baby can only thrive.

ANGELIC GUIDANCE

Let the true love that lives deep within me be communicated to the world and especially to my baby. I know tenderness is at the core of my being and is an expression of the love that lives in the spirit realm. Help me find the right tone, the most sensitive touch and the awareness to be with my baby. As I develop tenderness and compassion for my baby, I heal something deep within myself and this will let the angels and God's love come close to my heart.

Angelic Prayer

*Dearest Angel of Tenderness, please teach
me to love myself with the tenderness my
true nature deserves. No matter how
hardened I am, I know my tender, soft core
is a fundamental part of me. I want to
touch my baby from this tender place.
Help me accept my imperfections, hard
edges and all my limitations with
tenderness so that the deep well of love
within me can flow out. I want this
tenderness to embrace my baby. Thank you
for this blessing.*

 ## Meditation

*Feel the joy that comes from the love and
tenderness flowing through you. Look at
your baby with tender, soft eyes that
convey your love for him. Rock your baby,
coo to him and sing a sweet lullaby in a
tender, loving voice. Stroke his soft cheek
with your fingers and tell him how deeply
you love him. Each act of tenderness
allows you to build a foundation of love
that will last for a lifetime.*

37

CANCER BABIES

Your Cancer baby will change her moods as often as you change her nappies. Very compassionate and intuitive, she has a unique creative nature and is much affected by her experiences, which will leave strong visual and kinaesthetic imprints. She has a busy mind and is always recording and storing images. Her emotional needs are strong and her early home environment is very important. Like all Cancerians, she loves her home. It is her haven where she plays, feels safe and tries to live out her dreams.

ANGELIC GUIDANCE

I seek help in raising a well-balanced, loving and sensitive child who responds to the reality of life in a wholesome way. I know my child is caring at heart, loving and good but may find being disciplined and understanding boundaries difficult. Help me show my child how to overcome being too sensitive and to find equanimity in the face of challenges.

Cancer babies are oriented towards family life and are very dependent on the reactions of their parents and siblings. They enjoy attention but can turn melancholic when their focus is turned inward and they are dealing with their fears. This makes them vulnerable and somewhat fragile emotionally. When they are unsure, they will retreat into solitude and can become "crabby", feeling the world has let them down and making them disappointed in life.

Cancerians have a strong maternal side and they look after those they love. They have soft hearts but are cautious before giving both love and money. They carefully calculate their actions or experiences and like the assurance of an accepted outcome or financial security as a reliable foundation. They fear doing things alone and without an "insurance policy". Nearly all their ventures and projects turn out positively because they are not rash and exhibit a lot of careful forethought and planning.

Cancer babies are easy to manage and discipline, being generally docile and quiet. However, because they can easily get their way, if not monitored, they can become spoiled. They have a good sense of humour and love to laugh.

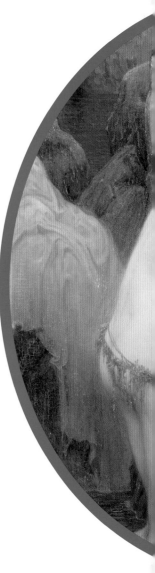

June 22nd - July 22nd

Cancerians are capable of great leadership with independent thinking and their own brand of individuality but need a lot of emotional empathy to develop their artistic and creative qualities. They have wonderful imaginations and make good artists, filmmakers and musicians. They like earning money and find jobs early in life where they can be paid.

Cancer babies have the possibility of growing into patient, generous and loving children but have a tendency to avoid the direct path towards their goals. They will walk sideways, like the crab they are named after, or around something but not go straight at it. They can be shy in expressing themselves and seldom show their inner desires but they love being cuddled and adored. If they don't get approval they feel crushed. These sensitive children can imagine hurts and slights and feel they are rejected. You need to take special care to convince your baby that she is good, smart, loved and wanted. A parent who can do this for his or her child will be honoured and loved into old age.

Traditionally minded, sentimental about the past and eager to collect old things, your Cancer baby will love animals and growing things, and being read to.

Dearest Angel of Cancer Babies, *please protect and guide my child to see the wholeness of life in truth, love and peace. I know my child has beautiful gifts that can serve the spirit of the world. Help us bring these out in our child in a loving and careful way.*

THE ANGEL OF Simplicity

"When I keep life simple, all complexity resolves itself. Baby and I love a simple day of love and bonding"

ANGELIC GUIDANCE

I seek to know what is really important for me and my baby. Help me create enough time to sit with my baby in a quiet and peaceful place, listen to beautiful music, read a good book, take a nap or cook a healthy meal. Help me avoid what is just fast and convenient and let me discover what is sincere and whole. I want to truly bond with my baby and form a creative and healthy foundation for the rest of our lives.

When you keep your life simple, you can more easily manage the tasks at hand. Having a new baby requires you to find practical and simple solutions to daily-care routines in order to free yourself from stress and find the time to enjoy your baby. It is easy to make your baby feel welcome, warm and comfortable; all you need to do is remove the negative, extraneous and complicated so you are able to focus on your baby.

Mums and dads who get enough rest, eat proper food and enjoy simple pleasures are happy parents. Babies whose days are kept easy, routine and rhythmic are also happy. All delight in simple activities like bath times or taking a stroll in the park. Simplicity, if it becomes integral to your way of life, can be a foundation of health and wholeness and can help you through demanding and complex changes. What is needed is to understand your priorities. When you become aware that your baby's needs come before anything else – at least in the first months – then a simple routine can be instituted that nurtures the entire family with its predictability and rhythm. Baby is always safe, comfortable and well cared for, and parents will have enough energy left over to manage their lives.

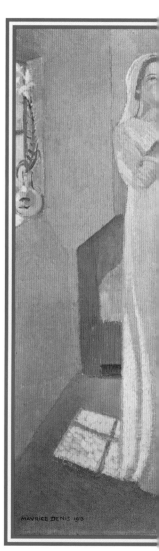

MAVRICE DENIS 1913

Angelic Prayer

Dearest Angel of Simplicity, please help me make the decisions that can simplify my life. Help me make choices for me and my baby that are healthy, sensible and practical and meet all our needs. I ask you to bless me with the awareness of what is simple, good and truthful for us all.

 ## Meditation

Take a moment to reflect on how you can bring simple innovations and a slower pace into your life. Is it important to be as social as you think you need to be? Are you content with your lifestyle choices? Do they support you in being happy and at peace with yourself? Do they give you quality time with your baby? If you choose to simplify your life what would you keep that works for you? How can you be a better parent, support your baby in his development and be happy?

41

THE ANGEL OF Tranquillity

"I live in tranquillity and allow love, joy and harmony to flow into my life and that of my family"

ANGELIC GUIDANCE

I seek help in creating tranquillity in my home. I know I can handle challenges with better balance and grace when I have the inner assurance that everything is as it needs to be. I want a greater sense of tranquillity in my life and this is a wonderful opportunity to begin establishing this. Please help me become tranquil so I can tune into the wise guidance of my life. I know you only await my request for help and guidance. I trust you to help me with my needs. I want a more tranquil, less dramatic existence where baby can safely rest and develop in a healthy way.

New parents worry and fret over their newborns. They are seldom relaxed or tranquil about their new situation. They bring anxiety home from work, lose sleep agonising over problems and create tension in the home, which, in turn, affects their babies. Some even obsess over every squeal and cry and become nervous over normal baby behaviour, making it challenging to differentiate when something is seriously in need of attention.

Cultivating an atmosphere of peace and tranquillity within oneself sets the tone for a happy and relaxed home. It makes it much easier to be a new parent. We all need to create a haven from the problems of the world and especially so when a delicate new soul has just entered the world. A new baby needs a shield of tranquillity in order to settle into and adjust to life.

It is possible to establish sufficient inner tranquillity so that when your baby does cry, you do not become irritated or frantic. Finding out what the problem is will help you understand your baby's sensitivities. You can become aware of the difference in cries and what they mean – distinguishing a cry for hunger or comfort from just a stretch of the lungs. Soothing your baby is an act of kindness and love and when it is done in a tranquil, loving manner it helps both you and your baby. Staying tranquil creates an atmosphere in which your baby can overcome his distress.

This is an opportunity to ask your angels for help. They can support you in creating a tranquil space where peace abides. Asking the angels to help you with a baby in distress can be a prayer answered. Allow the angels into your consciousness and they can whisper in your ear exactly what will help your baby relax. Angels support parents by helping them modulate their voices, to feel comfortable rocking or carrying their babies, and by knowing just what needs to be done to soothe a baby's delicate nervous system.

Angelic Prayer

....

Dearest Angel of Tranquillity, help me
develop tranquillity in all the things I do,
especially as I undertake the task of
parenting my new baby. Help me feel
tranquil so I can ease my baby's distress
and bring peace to his spirit. Help me
maintain a sense of evenness and balance
in my approach to all things concerning
my baby. I pray for calmness, peace and
tranquillity.

 # Meditation

Sit quietly for a few minutes at the
beginning and end of each day. In the
morning, you may want to read some
spiritual words, or reflect on what you
would like the day in front of you to be
like. You can see yourself and your baby
happy, contented and enjoying one
another. Bless the day that is coming to
you with gratitude. At the end of the day,
you will want to release it with the
conscious awareness that you had many
blessings throughout the day. Each day
you do this you gain in establishing a base
of tranquillity and inner peace.

Tranquillity helps everyone in the family. It helps each individual to ease down into a peaceful place, and this, ultimately, supports baby. You can create tranquillity through meditation, quiet music, gentle candlelight, even a hot bath. Look within yourself to find ways that encourage a sense of tranquillity to soften the rough edges of your life. Having a tranquil sense of things helps you stay centred when there is crisis.

Find a few moments every day to meditate and centre yourself before engaging with your baby and the world around you. This is very helpful and gives you a wholesome perspective for the long-term task of parenting.

THE ANGEL OF Ease

" I allow ease to permeate my life in every respect. Ease reflects my joy in parenting and my love of life"

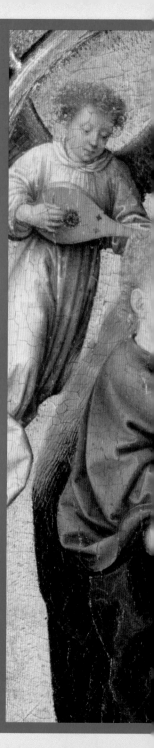

ANGELIC GUIDANCE

Please help me cultivate a real sense of ease as I look after my new baby. I would love ease to be a part of my life experience from now on. I call for ease to help and support my task of being a new parent, a loving partner and member of my community. I call on the angelic realm to help me develop an attitude of ease. This is new to my thinking and may require time to anchor in my consciousness. I am asking for guidance in bringing ease into all aspects of my life – relationships, work, finances and health.

Ease can define the way you live, love and relate to life. It can support you in the everyday events of your life. When you allow ease into your life you create a realm of possibility for your good to find you. Ease can help your baby feel the world around him is safe, loving and trusting. It will help in all your tasks and will dispel attitudes that life is a struggle and hardship necessary. Give yourself permission to let ease flow in your life and be the context with which all things unfold for you and baby.

Ease is an attitude; it is a lens through which we look at life situations and see whether the glass is half full or half empty. Ease is trust in the goodness of life and there can be no better message to pass onto your baby as he begins his life.

Ease says that everything is all right, even if it appears otherwise. It is a sense of alignment with your highest good that can guide you through rough waters helping you land in a safe haven. It fosters comfort, confidence and contentment. Ease is not how others respond to you but how you respond to the world around you, especially the chores of parenting. If you address the tasks of parenting with ease, the sting will be taken out of challenges.

Angelic Prayer

Dearest Angel of Ease, please bring ease into my awareness so that I am able to enjoy the goodness that flows to me. I know I am a being of love and that love is in and all around me. I know ease is a marker of that love. I choose to create ease as a beacon that flows before me in all my life situations. Help me transform my old thinking that was predicated on hardship and suffering to one of light, ease and joy. I pray for your help now and give thanks for your help.

 ## Meditation

Visualise what the day ahead of you looks like in your mind. Do you see it unfolding with ease? Can you add that element into the equation of the day? Picture yourself tending to your daily routines in a state of ease. See yourself smiling and happy. Feel you have the capacity to overcome distress. You can allow the idea of ease to enter your consciousness and work its way into your every act. You can call it to you in challenging situations. The more you do this the more control you have over your day and, ultimately, your life.

GODLY QUALITIES

This chapter focuses on the gifts of the spiritual realm – faith, love, trust and peace, which are available to parents and babies through the angels. You can call on these qualities to help fortify your courage and help you move forward in the process of parenting. The Angel of Faith teaches you to have faith in a higher power to see you through life; the Angel of Love is there to deepen your capacity to cherish another and be present for him or her; the Angel of Trust enables you to trust yourself as you undertake parenting and the Angel of Peace will strengthen your desire for a good, peaceful and loving life.

Being a parent entails many responsibilities. As well as living in a state of constant vigilance in order to keep an eye on baby, parents have to deal with all the practicalities of managing a home and, often, hold down a job as well. The fears, doubts and anger that can mount are great. All parents need the help of angels to see them through this challenging time.

Faith requires a belief in a power that is greater than our limited minds. It is the strongest human quality we are capable of cultivating and it allows us to turn over our problems and troubles and arrive at a better state of love and trust.

Love is what we are. It is the foundation and building block of the universe, the substance of life itself. When you have a new baby, love bubbles up from every cell in your body and expands to embrace your child and bless all around you. Love comes naturally to parents. The expression of your love is a living being in the form of your baby.

Trust that life will see you through provides you with a wholesome attitude that makes even insurmountable challenges figments of your imagination. Trust in life gives you the affirmative belief that you will get through the tough and difficult times and manage the challenges that face you and that ultimately, you will be fine.

And, finally, peace is the blessing that enables you to allow joy and goodness into your life.

These core qualities of faith, love, trust and peace require an internal awareness that you are absolutely connected to spirit at all times. There is never a moment you are not part of God or that God is not part of you. Your life is sacred, your child's life

is sacred. Your faith defines how you will move forward in life. Love is the quality that gives warmth, joy and fulfillment to your experiences. Trust is that bedrock of knowing that life is good and you are a part of it. Peace allows all the other qualities to flourish in your life.

The Tempe Madonna *by Raphael depicts the sanctity of love between mother and child. They rest against one another in a state of tender connectedness. Mother and baby have full faith that love abides. The Madonna appears trusting, at ease and open in her unguarded affection as she lovingly holds her baby to her cheek. Her baby's head is turned towards the world and his heart is held firmly against his mother's. This is a posture of love, an expression of faith, an act of total trust in the most peaceful of settings.*

THE ANGEL OF Faith

"My faith in life is affirmed by my baby"

Faith has been described as the substance of things hoped for, the evidence of things not seen. It takes faith to be a parent and to accept and know that a baby has her own life and own destiny. Of course, all parents want the best for their babies and it takes deep faith to know that each person receives her blessings of health, wholeness and happiness. Faith is the knowing this is so.

Faith teaches us that whatever happens in life is ultimately good. Trusting that we can traverse life's challenges deepens our faith and frees us from worry, self-punishment and fear. When you surrender to the guidance of the spiritual realm, you let a higher power act on your behalf.

Faith in life means you assume the power of love is always working on your behalf. This allows you to experience the world as safe, meaningful and loving, no matter what challenges occur. You will know all is well and that your challenges are for your healing and growth.

Faith frees you from the anxiety that you have to make it all happen and be in a state of constant alertness and control. Faith helps release the need for constant striving that grips so many people in our time.

Living in faith suggests that you do all that you are able to do for yourself and your baby. You develop faith and live in trust that your child is always looked after and guided. Faith can take you through illness, upsets and disruptions. Faith lights your way through the dark moments.

Faith develops because, for parents especially, it is impossible to be everywhere, on top of everything, all the time. Open your mind and heart to the love and support of the Angel of Faith, who can guide you towards truth and wisdom of acceptance and infinite patience.

Angelic Prayer

Dearest Angel of Faith, I pray that you can help me transform control, anxiety and fear into faith. Faith is my connection with the Source. It helps me know in my heart that I am loved, guided and protected at all times. Help me accept my highest good based on the faith that my baby and I can have good and happy lives. I trust that life will provide me with all our needs.

 ## Meditation

Look deep within yourself and call up your faith in life. You can allow it to deepen into gratitude and trust. In faith, you begin to experience that all is well and you are held in the arms of love. You may have many wishes that your baby be happy and healthy, and never want or need for anything. Have faith that life will give your child all she needs to grow, develop and become strong. Have faith that your baby will develop a good moral fibre. In your faith, you will be strong and able to meet all of life's challenges.

THE ANGEL OF Love

"I am made whole and alive by the power of love"

The Angel of Love is an unyielding force that holds you and your baby in its wings. Love is what brought your baby to you and as she begins her life's journey, be assured that the forces of love that guide and protect her will guide and protect you, too. The Angel of Love supports you in spite of your imperfections and errors of judgement and the doubts and fears that will naturally arise. Hopefully you will choose love over self punishment.

Love is the greatest gift we receive in life and is part of every human experience. It forgives all wounds, and is the sustenance that keeps us on track when we are confused and unsure. Love is what warms the soul and enables you to develop self-love, wholeness and compassion. Love promises wholeness, creativity, fun and delight. It brings out your sense of humour and it refines your parenting skills. It is what will heal all your old wounds.

Through challenges and losses, love will keep you going when you are hurt or disillusioned. It keeps you strong for necessary battles and steady during a crisis or illness. Allow it to find its place in your life.

Call on the Angel of Love in your daily experiences. When you feel depleted and tired from long nights, dirty nappies and the cries you can't soothe, ask this angel to help you receive love. Love will nurture you and feed you in times of despair and loneliness. It is always there, abiding deep within you. You simply open yourself to receiving it and allow it to flow into your heart.

Let love be what binds you to your child, not duty. Your baby feels she has been immersed in love in the spirit world and once born, love becomes the crucible in which she will flourish and thrive. Love lives in your baby and she will respond to it in you.

Choose love above all things. Let the Angel of Love bless you with its grace.

ANGELIC GUIDANCE

Help me find love within myself and enable me to express it outwardly to the world and especially to my baby. Let me understand that love is the ultimate gift we receive. When I choose love I say "yes" to God, and "yes" to life. Let love unite me with my child. I know that when I choose love, life triumphs.

50

Angelic Prayer

Dearest Angel of Love, I pray to you to release my fears, doubts and worries and eradicate any self-limiting attitudes, which negate my experience of love. I know my capacity for love affects my baby in every way. I pray to expand my ability to give and receive love and to shower my baby with warmth and goodness. Please help me stay positive, whole and affirming as I accept the role of parent.

 ## Meditation

Look at your baby and feel the outpouring of love that comes from her. She is a being of pure love. Experience the love that flows from your heart to your baby's heart and back to you. You'll realise that love is infinite and there is no beginning or end to it. Experience its rhythmic flow every day. Visualise it as a pink flow that expands daily. The more you love your baby, the happier, stronger and more vital she becomes.

LEO BABIES

ઠ

Leo babies have a life force that is strong and their will is apparent in all they do. Generally speaking, they are positive individuals and are often flushed with the glow of life. They are extroverts with strong personalities and great determination, and are rich in dignity and personal pride. Leos will work hard and play even harder. They are wonderful people to have around in an emergency; they readily take command and do not shirk their duty. They give advice to others naturally and make excellent educators, politicians and psychiatrists. They have a natural compassion for the weak and helpless.

The Leo child is sunny, happy, playful and always best when he gets his own way; if not, storm clouds will appear and he can become very sulky. It is not a good idea to suppress a Leo's enthusiasm or high spirits. Allow him to find himself and be a parent who creates wholesome boundaries that let him know you know.

Your Leo child will be a natural leader but teach him to let other children have their turns. A Leo can be bossy, usually commanding others what to do and how to do it. He also will have a strong sense of justice and you can point out the rules of fair play to him and he will grasp what they mean. He may, however, need to learn

ANGELIC GUIDANCE

Help me parent this child who appears larger than life at times and has us all enchanted by his charm, charisma and intelligence. I need to create balance so he learns the rules of fair play and can address others with kindness and compassion and to strengthen his inner resources so he can come to know himself in love, pride and assurance.

Dearest Angel of Leo Babies, thank you for the joy of this sunny child. Please protect him from accidents and keep him safe, alert and careful of his person. Help him find the balance between the inner and outer world so that his energy is conserved for a higher purpose and his heart is not always giving to others.

July 23rd - August 22nd

to respect others in order to receive their respect. Luckily, Leos are quick to learn and fast to perceive emotional truths.

Many little Leos can be ingratiating and charming but some love to show off. When this happens, you need to tell your child that showing-off is undignified as this will appeal to his Leo vanity and he will quickly curtail such behaviour. He will love being shown off at a very early age to friends and family and will graciously accept attention, gifts, flattery and adoration. This is not a child you need to coax into the limelight. That is his natural habitat. He is innately dignified and has a regal bearing which can create the impression, at a very early age, that he is kingly, but a spoiled Leo is a tyrant, so beware of over-indulging his ego.

Leos make loyal friends and are fun to have around. They respond well to continuous discipline and a great deal of love and affection. They have a powerful, creative energy that is strong and resilient.

A Leo's weakness is his recklessness and his laziness. A Leo loves to party and can be careless with money. Therefore, your child may need to learn to handle his finances; Leos can make and lose fortunes and be overly generous with others. They also can overdo things, become tired and end up needing to be coaxed into activity, especially outdoors.

This is not an easy child to raise because he will be hard to tame. He requires that you be vigilant, set strong boundaries and stick to them; harshness, however, will destroy a Leo's pride. Another problem is that a Leo child can be accident prone and experience sudden violent illnesses. Although generally strong and resilient in recovery, when ill, he will loathe bedrest and detest being coddled.

THE ANGEL OF Trust

*"I trust in love
and I trust in myself"*

Trusting life anchors love and goodness in the world. When you have a strong foundation of trust, you are better able to sustain equanimity through life's challenges. When you learn to trust in yourself, you will receive inner guidance that brings happiness and joy. Trust in life is synonymous with knowing your good is unfolding. It allows love to find you and to heal the world.

When a new baby is born, her soul needs to experience the goodness, stability and constant warmth she remembers from the angels. Love can provide this. You support your baby best by trusting in goodness and love and, especially, by trusting in yourself.

Without trust, life becomes riddled with anxiety and fear. You lose the sense of where you belong and how to respond to situations. If you don't have a healthy foundation of trust, you must begin to cultivate it and secure it in your consciousness. No one wants to remain a victim to life so its important to apply to the Angel of Trust to lose any negative thoughts.

Trust helps you establish a healthy and solid foundation for experiencing reality. It helps you understand life, rather than constantly needing to explain or control it. You are strengthened, made whole and blessed through trust. Trust allows you to transmit a deep sense of love and goodness to your baby in order to assure her that life is safe and all is well. This is the foundation that will allow her to enter the world in a good way.

Angelic Prayer

Dearest Angel of Trust, thank you for holding me steady and stable as I find my way as a parent. Thank you for helping me to put my trust in life as I take on this new experience. I realise that I have been given much to love and cherish. I ask for guidance to live a love-filled life full of trust in the good.

 ## Meditation

Reflect on trust. Do you trust in yourself? Can you reach deep within yourself to a place where your life merges with all life and where you know you are supported and cherished in spite of what your mind tells you? Are you able to find the truth, strength, wisdom and love that abide within. You can bring these qualities into your conscious life and help your baby sense that life is good and she is safe.

THE ANGEL OF Peace

*"Peace lives in my heart
and guides my life"*

Our hearts long for peace. When you bring a new child into the world you want your child to live in a world at peace. Peace should begin at home; home should be an environment that allows peace to hold baby's spirit so she can settle in and feel comfortable and easy with life. Let your home and heart be defined by peace. It is, in truth, a part of your very nature to experience peace.

Peace allows life to flow in its natural rhythms through our daily lives. It provides a stable and healthy environment in which a baby flourishes. It fosters a sense of security and wellbeing that enables your baby to grow and develop because it is safe to do so.

In truth, we can only relax from the tension of life's pressures when we allow peace in our hearts and minds. Peace lets us thrive; it nurtures our spirits, and is the underpinning of a loving and happy home.

When you seek the help of the Angel of Peace, you are asking for your baby to sleep better, eat better, and grow optimally. You

ANGELIC GUIDANCE

Help me create peace as the cornerstone of my existence. It is what baby and I need in order to thrive. I know peace is within me. I ask for your help in touching that place in my heart where it abounds, where all is well and where I can go when I am lost or unsure. Help me create a peaceful sanctuary where I can rest, relax and enjoy my baby.

56

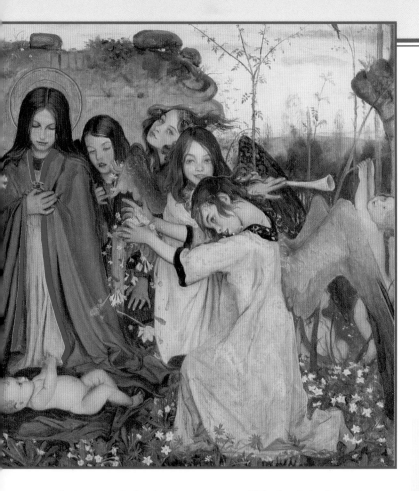

Dearest Angel of Peace, help me find the
core of my being where God's love
expresses itself as peace. I ask this for
myself and for my baby, who longs for
peace to begin her life on earth. Help my
baby thrive in a peaceful environment
where there is a steady flow of activity
marked by ease and tranquillity. We ask
that all non-peaceful aspects of our lives be
released and replaced with peaceful and
joyful activity. Place an aura of peace
around my baby to protect her.

 Meditation

Gently begin to sense that deep within
your heart is a deep well of peace. You can
tap into this at any time. It is yours to call
on whenever you feel unsure, unwanted or
lost. Peace is that gift that is always
available to you. Peace is the assurance
that all is well, all is good and all is love.

ask that your baby develops a sense of life that is joyful and
expansive and that conflict, disharmony or tension, which will
cause your baby to withdraw and close herself off from her
environment, be banished.

Peace lets us experience joy and pleasure. This does not mean
that everything is always quiet. Within peace there exists activity,
flow, order, harmony and humour. There is, however, a sense of
balance that pervades your life.

GIVING THANKS

Angels love our praise and thanks. That is their reward for their help and guidance. You can give back to them through honouring them in celebration and rejoicing, and by consecrating your baby to the highest principles of life. Through this you call the Angel of Celebration and Rejoicing to you and form a relationship with the Angel of Consecration. This, in turn, brings your spirit close to the Angel of Joy and the Angel of Fulfillment. You are blessing them as you find your happiness and sense of grace in being a parent and having a new baby.

Gratitude keeps you conscious of all the good that you have in your life. It reminds you that you take nothing for granted nor are you entitled to simply take the good that is presented to you. Gratitude is your way of acknowledging the many gifts you receive each day.

To deny the good because you feel you are entitled limits you and makes you a taker in life. To acknowledge the gift of life, the kindness of people, the beauty that surrounds you and, most particularly, the wonder of your new baby, is how you give back to the spirit world. You say

"Thank you, God, for this wondrous gift. Thank you, for the blessings that pour into my life."

If you were to make a list of the good you experience daily you would be shocked by how many wonderful things are given freely. Life itself is the greatest gift; your well-functioning body and your ability to see, hear and touch are amazing gifts. The beauty of the world around you is a gift, as is the love and kindness of the people you know.

To give thanks for a new baby provides you with the opportunity of fully expressing your humility and gratitude for your own life and the gift you have received. Remembering how precious this all is gives you a reason to give back to life in so many ways.

In Raphael's Constabile Madonna, *the Madonna contemplates a book setting out the law for the sacred act of the consecration of life – the ancient Jewish custom of honouring tradition and showing gratitude to God. The Madonna is still and calm. Her child, on the other hand, is playful and full of energy. One senses the mother knows she is truly blessed with a wonderful gift. Her baby is safe but, at the same time, very curious and aware.*

PART

5

THE ANGEL OF
Celebration and Rejoicing

*"I celebrate the birth of my baby
with joy and delight"*

Celebrating the birth of a healthy, beautiful baby is a way of offering thanks to the spiritual realm for the miracle of life. Whether this is done at a baptism or bris, or simply at a family gathering, you are introducing your baby to the angels and to your community of friends and family.

When you express your gratitude, the whole angelic realm delights in your joy and offers you their blessings. Gratitude acknowledges that you are delighted with the gifts your baby brings into your life. It honours the miracle you have received. Your home, family and community are blessed by this child.

Celebration announces to the world that you are humbled and made whole by your child. It is a sacred expression of your gratitude. You give thanks for being delivered of a healthy baby; you rejoice at the gift given. When you celebrate, you affirm your child's individuality and your responsibility in stewarding him to maturity. You also honour the spiritual and the Source of all creation who made this possible.

Rejoicing is a powerful expression of thanks to our Creator. You can call on the Angel of Celebration and Rejoicing to help you share your joy with those who know and love you and who wish you well as a parent. You know your baby brings the blessings of a lifetime to you.

ANGELIC GUIDANCE

Help me to create a wonderful acknowledgement of the miracle of life. Enable me to gather together those I love and with whom I wish to celebrate my good fortune of being blessed with the gift of this child. Help my family and friends to put aside any acrimony or hurt we may have experienced in the past and let us unite in the spirit of love. Help make our celebration of life joyful.

Angelic Prayer

Dearest Angel of Celebration and Rejoicing, please help me value the gift of life each day. In truth, I know that every day I share with my baby is something I want to acknowledge with thanks. When I see my baby grow, develop and thrive, I know this is a cause for celebration and rejoicing. I am blessed with my baby and ask the blessings of those who love us. I know this baby is a gift to me individually, and to my partner, family and community. Thank you for helping us celebrate this sacred occasion.

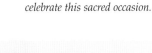 ## Meditation

Reflect on what would be an appropriate way to celebrate this new life. How would you create a ceremony that expressed your joy, gratitude and humility? Which beloved friends, family and colleagues will you invite to celebrate these new beginnings – you as a parent and your baby's life.

THE ANGEL OF Consecration

*"Life is sacred. I consecrate
it with a ceremony of love"*

Consecration is an act of acknowledging the blessings we receive. We consecrate our greatest joys as well as our losses. We treasure God's gift of life to us and are deeply grateful for having received this blessing. What could bring greater joy than to welcome a new child into life and acknowledge its source?

You may wish to consecrate your baby's life to spirit in the hope that he will mature into a responsible and spiritual being. This is an ancient way of offering thanks for being. Whatever form your consecration may take – be it a traditional ceremony or a personal ritual shared with friends and loved ones, offering up your thanks is a humble and heartwarming act of gratitude. In doing this, you ask that your child's life be protected and guided. You acknowledge where life comes from and that it has blessed you with grace, guidance and love.

An act of consecration is a sacred gesture. It is a direct acknowledgement of the power of love your child symbolises. It may consist of a simple prayer or reading an appropriate poem aloud. It could be a song that celebrates the life of this new child. Call upon the Angel of Consecration for inspiration. You can make your act of consecration as embellished as an official sacrament in a church or temple or as simple as offering up a whisper of a prayer of thanks. What truly matters is your avowal of gratitude for the blessing received and that you acknowledge with reverence that life is sacred.

Your prayers for your child's life should centre on his being welcomed, honoured, blessed and accepted by those who watch over him and are stewards for his welfare. Each prayer for his health, happiness, prosperity, creativity, love and joy carries a wish that life be good and your baby remains safe.

ANGELIC GUIDANCE

Help me create an appropriate ritual and ceremony that honours my baby and his relationship to the Creator. I acknowledge the power of Spirit in our lives and wish to share this with people close to me. Consecration is a sacred act of acknowledgement and gratitude, which I can use to launch my baby into the world. As he grows and matures, he will have a strong and indelible connection to the spirit world that will connect him to his angels and to the earth.

Angelic Prayer

Dearest Angel of Consecration, thank you for this opportunity to offer up thanks for the blessings this new baby brings into my life. I know that I am blessed and humbly acknowledge this miracle of life. I know that every prayer and good wish helps my baby feel safe and welcome. I delight in honouring the gift of life that inspires my joy. I know this is a sacred act.

 ## Meditation

Sit with your baby in your arms and quietly form a thought of gratitude in your heart that consecrates the life of your child. Offer up your prayers to God and the angels in thanks for the blessings you have received with your baby. All pain, suffering and trauma are released in this moment of acknowledgement.
The gift of life is given to you to love, cherish and protect.

VIRGO BABIES

Virgos are quiet, often singular, studious and methodical. Some call them perfectionists. Neat and tidy, precise, meticulous, practical, dependable and conservative by nature, they are conscientious with a strong sense of obligation. They are often chosen for teacher's pet because they accept discipline and are good students. If, however, too much emphasis is put on mistakes, this may create tension in the little Virgo child, who will worry too much about being perfect.

ANGELIC GUIDANCE

Please help my child develop imaginative skills, and balance the practical, grounded life ordained for a Virgo child with a rich, inner fantasy life that can sustain and nourish his soul. Help me show my child all sides of a situation where there is both a realistic and practical aspect as well as magical and mythical possibilities that can enchant and delight. Help my child see the inner and the outer, the dark and the light and accept all without criticism or judgement.

August 23rd - September 22nd

Beloved Angel of Virgo Babies, Please guide my child to know the truth about life and to never turn away from discovery because his imagination is inactive. Support the practical and open the magical as possible paths to the same conclusions that life is worthwhile and my child is a welcome part of it.

Virgo babies talk early and have a wonderful sense of mimicry. They can copy you in most of your gestures and actions and make very good actors because of this trait. They are very alert and quick yet peaceful and tranquil. This means they can soothe and irritate at the same time. They are generally pleasant children who have few tantrums and engage in little conflict. They can form strong habits early on; for example, they will develop their own eating schedules and can be very fussy about their food.

Virgos can be bashful and shy. They are friendly with family and friends but wary of strangers. Seldom troublesome, they make wonderful companions and thrive on physical affection. They are good with pets, who teach them how to love quietly, and at caring for the helpless, ill and infirm.

With a stronger sense of duty than a love of frivolity, Virgos are too busy with their projects to spend time daydreaming and may need work in developing their imaginations. They are not fond of fairy tales or make believe because these challenge their perceptions of reality. They know where they are all the time and respond to kindness in a conservative way, holding back in affection and being careful about spending money. Their greatest flaw is how self-critical they can be with themselves.

You can count on Virgos to get a job done; they work harder and longer at projects than other sign but worry about not getting the job done, failing and not being dependable.

They thrive on bringing order out of chaos and hate waste. Unfortunately, their nervous systems react to this precision and they often suffer with upset digestions.

65

THE ANGEL OF Joy

*"I connect to the deep well
of joy within me"*

The joy of having a new baby goes deep into your heart. It remains in spite of all the work demanded of new parents. Babies nurture us because they are pure joy. They come to us fresh from the angels. The Angel of Joy can help you remain in a state of joy while meeting the challenges of parenthood.

A new baby allows you to share your joy with others. He is, after all, a symbol of hope in the future and reconciliation with the past. He is a link to the oneness of all life. In your heart you know there is nothing more joyful than your baby, who offers the world new hope and you a new beginning and chance for healing.

Each time you hold your baby or look into his eyes, you can feel your heart fill with joy. You can feel it when you bathe him, change his nappy, play with him and nurse him. You are made whole by the experience of love that you feel for your new baby. Babies evoke joy!

Babies represent the common love for life we all share. They remind us of what is good, tender, pure and uncomplicated. Few creatures on earth have as much power to make people smile, laugh and feel good about life than a new baby. We are all so grateful for this.

ANGELIC GUIDANCE

Help me to always enjoy a loving heart and a grateful mind when I contemplate my baby and, for that matter, any baby. Let me be aware constantly that I am blessed by the pure love my baby brings to the world. Help my family find the joy in my new baby. Let me, as a young parent, experience the fact that I am blessed and protected.

Angelic Prayer

Dearest Angel of Joy, connect me to the source of joy that comes with new life. Help me remember that once I was a source of joy to my family and was loved and cherished in the same way as this new baby is cherished now. I ask to be reunited with that joy deep within me and to know that joy is a mainstay of life.

 ## Meditation

See if you can open your heart to the pure joy that lives within you and resonates within your baby. See how he responds to your attention with bright, inquisitive eyes and a sweet smile. Let yourself be warmed by the goodness and purity of your baby. You can be touched by this beautiful source of joy every day in many different ways. Stay open to joy as much as possible. It will heal you.

THE ANGEL OF Fulfillment

"I am fulfilled by the expression of love I experience as a parent"

Fulfillment comes with the awareness that your baby represents something you longed for to make your life complete. As you give thanks for your new baby, allow yourself to feel a sense of deep fulfillment. Take time to absorb the thrill that being a parent is what you wanted and achieved. You anticipated this child's coming for a long while. Now, his arrival signifies the fulfillment of a dream come true.

There will be times when you will forget how you longed to be a parent or have a child and at those times, the Angel of Fulfillment can remind you of the special place your child has in your heart. However, for right now, focus on the awareness that you are fulfilled. Enjoy all the feelings of creative accomplishment and pride that come with having birthed a baby. Now you are a parent with a beautiful new baby. This child's life will unfold in love and he will become a mature individual thanks to all the efforts you will make on his behalf. Enjoy the feelings and experience how deep your fulfillment runs. It will help you grow and mature as an individual.

Angelic Prayer

*Dearest Angel of Fulfillment, I
acknowledge that something deep in my
soul has blossomed in being a parent and
welcoming this beautiful baby into my life.
This relationship fulfills something so deep
within me I cannot express it in words.
Help me to tap into my inner core to
remember this feeling. Let it carry me
forward throughout my life. I know it
makes me more loving and compassionate.*

 ## Meditation

*Turn silently inward to your deep centre.
Allow yourself to experience a deep sense
of fulfillment and happiness that you have
a new baby. Allow yourself to feel the joy,
pride and the wonder of it all. Life is a
great mystery and as a new parent you are
a part of it. Acknowledge to yourself and
those you love how deeply fulfilled you feel
holding and loving your baby. This
enriches your soul's life and fortifies the
bond between you and your baby.*

UNCONDITIONAL ACCEPTANCE

As a parent, you now have the opportunity to explore the possibility of spiritual growth through the Angel of Unconditional Love. This gift will open your heart and mind to the truth of love for who you are and who your baby is.

Through the Angel of Warmth and Care, you focus the depth of love within you into your baby, creating a channel of love that will be indelible and permanent, no matter what happens in life.

As you become more content and practised as a parent, you can call the Angel of Serenity into your life to help you feel the truth of ease and calmness that helps baby grow and thrive and that can transform your life and help you internalise your world more.

It is through the Angel of Flexibility that you become a realistic parent, able to adapt to changes, able to be clear about what needs to be done and to forge your path as a parent with your own unique sense of what works for both you and your baby.

Unconditional acceptance comes from the core of your being. It is not touched by the critical and discerning nature of the mind. It is a heartfelt quality that pervades and excuses everything. You may wonder if it requires you to be a saint. In fact, it demands more of you than sainthood. Unconditional love requires that you be a loving and devoted parent.

Unconditional acceptance is not natural to us. We learn about it through watching our parents interact, in playing with friends and by loving pets. To completely accept another human being without judgement, conditions or qualification, could be one of the most difficult tasks you face as a human being.

Loving your child in the perfection of her being, exactly as she is, without adding anything or taking anything away, is what elevates your spiritual essence. It is what helps every baby grow and thrive. It has more sustenance than actual food and greater potency than any medicine or vitamin you can take.

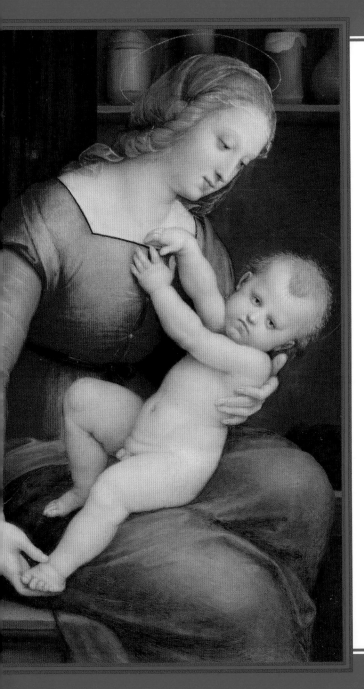

Unconditional acceptance means complete complicity with and delight at everything your baby is, does or expresses. With it the first twelve months of life can become an idyllic experience for any child. After that time, however, boundaries get put in place and life's realities become known.

Everyone should be entitled to a perfect babyhood. It gives immunity against the challenges that will come in life and provides a resiliency that is uncontestable in the face of illness and stress. After a perfect babyhood, parents need to address other issues regarding educating and training. Once a baby becomes mobile and capable of reaching out to the world, the parameters become more harshly defined, and rightly so. No one can stay a baby forever. But while your child is young, the only rule that applies is total and abounding unconditional acceptance.

In Raphael's painting of the Virgin of the House of Orleans, *the young mother sits in a silent and still repose holding her child in her lap. One of his feet rests on her hand. The baby gently touches the top of her gown. The mother's gaze is intently focussed on her child and is full of unconditional love. This will bond them as mother and child through eternity.*

THE ANGEL OF Unconditional Love

"I receive the gift of unconditional love from my baby and I return it fully"

ANGELIC GUIDANCE

Please guide me towards full acceptance and unconditional love for my baby. It is not easy to love unconditionally and to learn to non-judgemental. I want to be capable of this level of love. I know harsh judgements create separation and stifle creativity and the love of exploration and adventure. They limit one's ability to reach out to the world. Please help me follow the course of unconditional love and let it take me to a better place within myself.

Unconditional love means just what it says. It means you love without judgement, criticism or qualification. You love and accept your child exactly as she is. This gives your child permission to be who she is and you permission to be who you are.

Unconditional love is a rare gift you can receive from those close to you. There is no condition that you need to submit to in order to be loved. This is something that allows you to thrive, embrace your differences and know you are worthy of love. You know you belong. Unconditional love lets you experience yourself as a perfect specimen of God's love.

When you love your child unconditionally, you create an aura of total acceptance in which she can flourish. There is no criticism or lack that will make your baby feel she is wrong in any way. By allowing yourself to love at this deep level, you transform the way you accept and love yourself and the world around you. This level of love is what gives your child permission to be whom she is without having to change a thing about herself.

To love unconditionally is not easy; it is, however, what is asked of us. Few of us have ever experienced being loved unconditionally and our models are few. Often our judgement blocks our true perception of the godly qualities that are intrinsic in each person. When you can love your baby unconditionally, you create the context that allows your baby to encounter a world in which anything is possible.

Angelic Prayer

*Dearest Angel of Unconditional Love,
please help me cultivate a deep and
abiding capacity for unconditional love.
Help me release punishing judgements and
harsh criticism, restricting fears and
overbearing opinions that limit my child's
full expression of herself. These separate
me from the world and make it harder for
my baby to rise above these imposed
limitations. Help me love and accept my
baby unconditionally and, in turn, myself.*

 ## Meditation

*Watch your baby sleep. See her perfection,
beauty and grace. She is so new to the
world having come from the spirit realms
where she played with angels and was
loved freely and unconditionally. Let the
love you feel for your child permeate your
being; open your heart and allow love to
flow through you to your baby and the
world around you. This is a meditation for
years to come.*

THE ANGEL OF Warmth and Care

"My warmth and care embrace and nurture my baby"

Babies need warmth and care for their soul forces to thrive. They need this as much as they need food and shelter. When the atmosphere around them is replete with soul warmth, their spirits expand and their awareness of the world is whole and healthy. They feel safe and loved.

All beings expand in love and contract in pain. Your baby's nervous system is delicate and sensitive so you will want to create an atmosphere of complete protection for her. The Angel of Warmth and Care can give you guidance.

Warmth and closeness are life affirming and give a great sense of safety to a newborn. But babies also need conscious stimulation. Your baby will like to hear the sound of your voice and she can recognise it from her months in utero. She can also recognise other familiar voices such as Dad's.

When there is too much stimulation, your baby's responses automatically close down; when there is not enough, she will become torpid and inactive. Finding the right balance for her is a result of your care and attention to her needs. You should seek the harmonious point that gives your baby the optimal amount of stimulation, warmth and love. Learning to be aware of what your baby needs comes with time. Eventually, you will know what delights your baby and what disturbs her.

Most babies love to be rocked because it soothes their nerves and creates a reliable rhythm they enjoy. They also love the warmth of skin and the feel of soft, strong arms supporting them. Speak to your baby in soft, soothing words; this will help her pay attention to whomever is present and supports her development. Because babies do not do well when they are exposed to noisy environments, it should benefit your newborn to be in her warm, safe home so she can expand her perceptions without fear.

Meditation

Think about how you can make your baby feel she is beautiful, loved and welcomed. Are you using a soft tone of voice to express your warmth?. The more you do so the more she will become soothed and your soul warmth will permeate her being. Do you touch your baby gently and softly and massage her after her bath? Your baby will get to know herself through your conscious, loving touch.

Take time to pay attention to your baby, not just meet her demands for food or nappy changing. Your baby needs to experience your soul warmth and know that you care about her from your very being, not just because she has needs you are busy taking care of. She needs to know she is cared for at the deepest level of her being. Talking to your baby, playing with her and being close will help her settle into life in a good way.

LIBRA BABIES

Dearest Angel of Libra Babies, please bless our child with a sense of truth and fairness. Help her to find her way in the world with her intelligence and gift of honesty. I know that this child has great charm but I hope she comes to rely more on her intelligence than the ability to please others. Help us create a wholesome and healthy child ready to meet responsibility with grace and ease.

Librans have two dimensions to their personalities: they can be light and dark, loving and domineering, adorable and argumentative, good natured and pleasant but also sulky and disdainful of taking orders, intelligent but also gullible and naïve. They can be wonderful listeners but often monopolise the conversation by talking non-stop. Full of the duality of life that requires both ends of the spectrum to achieve balance, Librans perform a delicate balancing act to keep these conflicting character traits in perfect harmony. Half the time they are wonderful, charming, balanced and calm, and the other half of the time they can be depressed, confused, restless and stubborn. First they are up, then they are down.

Libran children are good at softening hard hearts. They are charming and often get their way from a very young age. When they are raised with proper balance they are a delight. If they are spoiled before they attend school there will be problems. They need support but not coddling. These are children who truly want to please but must have harmony. When an adult forces them into a mould, they can become depressed and melancholic.

Libran children are born with bright, curious and logical minds that seek the truth. They are gifted with intelligence and have the ability to ponder deep subjects. Kind-hearted and fair, they like to know both sides of an issue. They are law abiding as long as they agree that the law is correct; the scales must always be balanced.

They are musical and artistic and have a great need to express themselves. They are excellent communicators and they do this through speech and smiles. They love to dress up and use products that make them feel good. They love harmony, peace, beauty and comfort to a high degree.

A Libran's worst habit is indecisiveness, which can lead to confusion and frustration. Your child will hate making decisions because she is afraid of making mistakes and hurting someone's feelings. From a very early age, she may struggle to choose colours, which sock to put on first and which delicious thing to begin eating. To parent your Libra baby well, never confuse her with too many options. Give her solutions over and over again until she thinks she has thought something out. At mealtimes, put only one thing at a time in front of her. The less decisions a Libran has to make, the happier she feels.

Librans have strong reactions to discordant interruptions and emotional trauma and suffer from sudden noises, loud sounds and harsh colours. They need peace and quiet. It is important never to invade a Libran's privacy.

Librans enjoy activity and then a good rest to restore their vitality. If they play hard, they must rest hard. It is the only way they can stay healthy. They need ample down time to match their active and, somewhat hectic, lives. It helps to understand this side of Libra so you can help your child avoid becoming too tired or worn out from overwork. Librans often have a very good instinct for their mental welfare and try to stay physically fit. They are healthier than most signs unless they push themselves too hard and forget how important rest is for them.

Librans can be excessive in many things, such as food and drink and their affections, and the biggest threat to their health is over-indulgence. It will be best to instill in your child a strong sense of self-discipline to help her overcome this weakness.

THE ANGEL OF Serenity

"I am always serene and calm with my baby"

Creating a calm and serene environment for yourself and your baby will help you both to thrive and flourish. Call on the Angel of Serenity to create a nest where you feel safe, at ease and happy, and that gives you a haven from all the stress and tension of the outside world. You may wish to furnish your space with a chair in which you can rock your baby or a cradle in which she can sleep feeling its rhythmic movements. Such a space helps to make your baby feel safe and cozy, which makes the jobs of parenting much easier. Serenity is as much a physical space as it is a state of mind.

You also can create uninterrupted time with baby where you could play together and strengthen your bond of intimacy and trust. Nothing is sweeter than to look at one another and share moments of love and delight. Such moments soften and warm your heart and fortify your baby's resolve to be in the world.

Quiet moments when you can meditate can provide serenity. As you deepen your faith in spirit and trust in life, you become more serene. Serenity is something a baby knows when she is in your arms. She basks in the glow of your essence. This helps you maintain a sense of serenity and an awareness that all is well in your life.

Angelic Prayer

Dearest Angel of Serenity, you are always present in my life. I need only call on you to remember to feel serene and accepting. It is always my choice to place this consciousness before me. There are many changes that come with being a new parent and I pray to you to help me transform my focus from the externals to a more internal awareness so I can support my baby in her growth and development and make our home a happy, serene place for all of us.

 ## Meditation

Visualise a violet glow around you and your baby. This is the colour of serenity. It holds and encapsulates you in an aura of protection, peace and tranquillity. Allow the serenity to enfold you and permeate your being. It fills the room you are in and your entire home. It makes everything you do and all that is asked of you easy, gracious and delightful. It makes your baby happy.

THE ANGEL OF Flexibility

"Acceptance deepens in me with every new day. I am flexible and adapt to change easily"

ANGELIC GUIDANCE

Help me look at a new challenge with a healthy perspective to make the right choices for my baby. Encourage me to adapt to change and be flexible. If I remain rigid my spirit stagnates and I miss the opportunity of learning from my experiences. There will be new options to choose among; help me see what is best for my baby and best for myself.

To truly accept changes a new baby brings into your life requires flexibility. If you have expectations about how you think life has to be with a new baby, you will need to adapt to inevitable changes. Flexibility will help you to manage the changes that are bound to happen. It will help you have an open mind and an eager heart for seeing your baby happy and well.

If you are fixed in your patterns and cycles, you need to develop a new rhythm that accommodates your baby. This is not easy, especially if you are trying to be as good as your own mother or "do" parenting like it says in the books. Allowing yourself to be flexible will help you adapt, and accommodate whatever emotions rise to the surface of your mind. Then you can accept the situation at hand, whatever it stirs up within you and be in the moment.

Part of growth is to bend to the reality of change and to address a situation by finding ways in which you can adapt. It helps you to stay mindful and to ask for the help needed to make the changes required of you. If you face the challenge of illness or simply adjusting to your baby's rhythm, you may need more flexibility to find the best path to follow. If you live with rigid ideas about parenting, you will miss the opportunity to make conscious choices about how to transform all new situations. Your baby asks that you be willing to pay attention to her rhythms and cycles, not to what a book says is correct, or even what you are told by others.

Flexibility may be as simple as asking the simple question, "What is best for my baby?" or turning to the Angel of Flexibility for help. Once you allow yourself to meet new situations, you are on the right track of flexibility. You are being real about parenting.

Angelic Prayer

Dearest Angel of Flexibility, please help me adapt to the situations I face as a parent. I want only to do what is best for my baby and I know fear, doubt and mistrust often prevent me from choosing what will support her in the long run. Help me be flexible in finding solutions that will ease my tasks and that serve the true needs of my baby. If there is something I need to know that will help me make a better decision for our welfare, lead me to it.

 ## Meditation

Sit quietly and hold your hand over your heart. Whisper to yourself that you love and totally accept your new life as a parent. Ask your angels to guide you to the best solutions for your baby's health and welfare. Ask yourself if you can be flexible and develop new ways of parenting. You'll find the answers you need within you. Do your best to release old, rigid ideas and adapt to new ways that help you be a better parent.

EARTHLY ANGELS

As a parent or relative of a new baby you are asked to welcome this new soul into the world, help him acclimatise to his new environment and help him feel safe. If you are his mother, you are generally required to be his primary caregiver and nurturer and sole sustenance. A mother thus has an essential, immediate role as well as a long-term commitment to educate and help her baby develop. She is asked to give support and care and when necessary, healing.

Every other loving relation of a baby helps to make him welcome. Each has a responsibility to honour the role that has been thrust on him or her or that has been assumed. These loving relations also exist to support the mother so that she may provide the best possible care imaginable for baby.

Each relationship baby has is blessed by an angel. There is an angel for mother, father, sisters, brothers, grandparents, godparents, aunties and uncles. Each of these roles is unique and carries an angelic blessing to unfold as baby comes in intimate contact with each person.

If you are one of the above, you can act as an angel in this baby's life. You can help him see the world as safe, fun, interesting, sane, productive, creative and worthwhile. You will set the standard for baby's initial and primary experience of the world. Angels bound to this world can provide support and help and they should make it easy for each member of baby's family and his friends to care and love one another as well as baby.

Every baby wants a happy family and often babies come to help mend rifts that have separated people from one another. They, too, are earthly angels.

Raphael's beautiful painting, The Holy Family of the Oak Tree, *depicts love and family unity. The relationship between the figures is intimate, trusting and affectionate. Mother gazes adoringly at her playful child whom she restrains on her lap while the child and his father exchange loving glances. St. John the Baptist, looks towards his cousin with brotherly regard.*

PART

7

Mother

"I affirm that I am a wonderful, loving and caring mother, doing the best I am capable of for my beloved baby"

As a mother you are the source of life for your child. You provide the space and nutrition for your baby to grow and thrive physically. You are the spiritual connection that allows your baby to experience the love of life and the spirit realm. How you regard this great task of being the centre of the universe for your baby can become a great spiritual awakening for you. You are the link that connects your baby to life.

Know that your angels are watching over you, protecting and nurturing you and your baby. They love you both and offer you their guidance and care. Allow them to be a source of great love for you both. The angels care for your welfare. They offer help and healing. Call on them when you need help. They can see you through the most challenging of times.

Being a mother requires strength, constancy and an abiding trust in yourself to do all the right things to protect and take care of your baby. As a mother you'll find that the angels will form a particular bond with you in the common purpose of looking after your baby. Know in your heart that you are looked after and all is provided for you. Allow yourself to receive the blessings that are there for you.

ANGELIC GUIDANCE

Think about what you need to help you in your tasks as a mother. Open your mind to the possibility that you do not have to feel burdened by doing everything alone. Often the invisible helpers we know as angels provide us with the gifts we need to have our good unfold. Ask them for help. They will respond graciously. They only long to be asked.

Angelic Prayer

*Beloved Angel of All Mothers, watch over
my baby, protect him, and guide me to be
in the right place at the right time to see
that all my child's needs are properly met.
Help me to ask for what I need to make
this task easier and to keep me strong,
healthy and safe for the sake of my family.*

 ## Meditation

*Being a mother may be one of the most
challenging jobs in life. Few people
acknowledge mothers for the work they do
and yet, they do not do it for the praise.
Know that you are doing your best as a
woman and a mother to provide the care
and sustenance your baby needs.
Acknowledge yourself for the choice you
made to become a mother, and honour
your need for help and support. Tell
yourself that you are a good mother.*

85

Father

"I love my baby. I provide all the love and care I am able. I stand by my child. I stand by my family"

ANGELIC GUIDANCE

I seek help in undertaking my new role as father and adjusting to the changed family circumstances. Show me how to meet my baby's needs and to know how best to take care of my baby and his mother. Let me be helpful in helping my child develop his full potential and enable me to set a good example for mature and responsible behaviour. Help me to be a loving source of strength to all who need me and teach me to trust that my instincts are right and sound. Show me how to see to my child's welfare, to be there when he needs me and to respond appropriately.

As a new father, you may be bewildered by the eventful changes in your life. Your baby requires attention and care, and you are no longer your partner's main focus of attention. Sharing in the responsibilities of parenting, however, will help you bond with your child and gain the respect of your family.

Traditionally, fathers built the fires that protected the camp, stayed up late listening for strange noises and watching out for unusual activities, and dealt with both animal and human intruders. They hunted for food and were the single source of welfare for mothers and babies. Today, however, both parents may share household tasks while each holds down a job.

With women in the work force and both parents striving in life, the role of fatherhood is being redefined. It will still fall on you to be the protector of your family and, possibly, its main breadwinner but you also may wish to help in other ways. Changing nappies, taking baby out in his pushchair or carrying him on your back will make you a much more hands-on dad and a valuable help to your partner. There are pleasures as well as responsibilities to be gained in such tasks as feeding and bathing a baby.

It's a wonderful thing to care for your child but you may need help with learning how to do the things that will benefit your family. Call on the angelic realm to help you focus your attention on being a loving and supportive father. If you ask them, the angels can help you do the job of protecting your baby, taking responsibility for his welfare and being an effective and efficient father and loving partner.

Angelic Prayer

Beloved Angel of Fathers, watch over me as I keep a watchful eye. Keep me safe, protected and able to respond when my baby is threatened in any way. Help me grow, mature and develop into an ideal parent and to accept my responsibilities. Ensure that the love I feel for my baby will keep me receptive to the demands that are being asked of me.

 # Meditation

So much is asked of a father. It is not an easy role to take on and you may need to grow into it gradually. As a father, you are asked to help take care of your baby, be present for and respond to your partner and usually do a day's work as well. If you take time to organise yourself so that there is time for your work, baby, partner and yourself, you may just about manage this juggling act. Stay aware of and flexible to change and open to truly communicating your needs so you can do manage things for the long term. Be alert to what needs doing in the moment and keep a sympathetic ear open to helping your partner find her way as a mother. You are bound to succeed. The angels bless you for your choice to be a parent and to step up to the plate of responsibility.

SCORPIO BABIES

♏ Scorpio babies have a maturity beyond their years and an intensity about them that will deepen into a strong intelligence and keen perception as they grow. They have a powerful physical strength and electric vitality. Even as babies you will notice their strong, sturdy frames.

A Scorpio's inner nature is often passionate and intense but well concealed under a quiet and gentle exterior. He will have trouble managing the intensity of his feelings and can be volatile but able to control his emotions with careful guidance. Your child will be highly sensitive and require privacy. He will want to know about the important aspects of life.

As a parent, you will be required to set strong guidelines and firm boundaries. Your Scorpio child will do well with constant and firm discipline. You can teach him to be considerate of those weaker than himself, how to be a good sport when he loses, and to forgive those who have hurt him or done him an injury.

As you help develop your child's character you will come to know he is very intelligent and has a magnetic personality. A Scorpio shows courage and honesty and is worthy of your greatest efforts to protect and nourish his spirit. Scorpios tend to learn only from those stronger than themselves and your child will admire you for your strength and ability to resist him. Add a lot of love and tenderness to your relationship, and you will experience a depth of love and loyalty not exhibited by other signs. Scorpio is the most loyal of children; he doesn't forget kindnesses done to him. Nor does he forget hurts and injustices and may seek revenge for any damage done him.

ANGELIC GUIDANCE

Please guide me in parenting this child who has such strong passions and intensity. I need strength in setting the boundaries that will guide my child into wholesome awareness about what is good and heals and what is bad and destroys. I ask for your vigilance in keeping us aware of where our child's curiosity takes him and when the forbidden is calling to him. I know we have a beautiful soul in our care. Please help us nourish it and guide it to responsible adulthood.

October 23rd - November 21st

Scorpios are born knowing the secrets of life and are wise about the mysteries. When they set their minds on achieving something, they are able to overcome all obstacles to have what they want. They seem to be able to turn their desires into reality through strong intention and clarity of mind. As a parent, it is best to guide your Scorpio child away from his fascination with what is unwholesome and forbidden. Keep him active physically and engaged mentally. He needs opportunities to work out his high energy. Help him channel his passion and curiosity into science, literature and sports.

Scorpios can be strange and enchanted children who have a destiny to fulfill that may require many experiences before this happens. Offer your love, constancy and support so that your child knows he does not walk the path of life alone. Give strong support for giving and accepting love.

Dearest Angel of Scorpio Babies, I pray that my child realises his higher nature and serves humanity with grace, courage and tenacity. Help our child find warmth and love as well as strong boundaries that will serve to guide and mould his character. Help us parent with love, firmness and great care.

89

Sisters

"I love my baby brother or sister with all my heart. I cherish this new being whom I will love and protect all my life"

Sisters are a gift to mothers and fathers. As a sister, you bring love, companionship and wholesome fun for your new sibling. Don't you marvel at this new being who has come into life to be a friend and companion to you throughout your life? As a good sister, you will love holding, feeding and playing with baby. It comes naturally to you to want to be and do what your mother does. You will realise that one day you, too, may choose to become a mother and care for a baby in the same way as your mother is doing now.

Being a big sister carries respect. The new baby will learn to feel safe and loved by you. He or she is thankful to have a friend so close at hand for times of love and fun.

As an older sister, you can sometimes be a source of strength when baby is having a difficult time and you can learn to soothe

ANGELIC GUIDANCE

As a big sister, I seek to look after and guide my new baby brother or sister as he or she grows up. I can be as good as a second mother and help baby and my mother when she is busy. I can understand baby's needs easily and care for him or her just like my mother does. Help me to realise what a precious gift I am to this new baby. Help me support and care for this baby as I would like to do with my own child when I am older and can choose to be a mother.

your little brother's or sister's temper and help him or her feel at peace. For a baby, having an older sister to pave the way in life is a gift and a blessing

Angelic Prayer

Dearest Angel of Sisters, bless me as I take on the role of being the older sister. Help me to realise what a gift I bring to this new baby who may be bewildered by life on earth. As a big sister, I want to learn to care for baby and participate in the role of caretaker. I feel responsibility for this baby's wellbeing. I know that he or she requires love, attention and care. Help me put away my rivalry for mother's attention and feel how appreciative mother is to have a responsible helper looking after baby with her. It is a big role and I need your help to do it well.

 ## *Meditation*

Being a big sister is a big responsibility for me. I need to set a good example for my younger sibling and be concerned to love and cherish him or her in all the right ways. I must learn to share my toys and activities. To be a help, I must learn to listen carefully to my mother and be careful around baby. I must remember to share my pride with my father when he asks how I am and what I did during day. If I care for my new brother or sister lovingly, everyone will acknowledge what a wonderful big sister I am. I know I am appreciated for my love and concern.

Brothers

*"I share my fun, enthusiasm
and joy with my sibling and
I protect those I love
as best I can"*

As a big brother, you will be a great ally in helping your new baby brother or sister discover the world. You may not pay this new baby a lot of attention at first, because you are busy with your own adventures and fun, but as your new sibling grows into a more receptive companion, you will enjoy his or her companionship and learn to experience love and gratitude for this new family member. You will act as a blessed guardian to your brother or sister, always vigilant to protect, guide and share with him or her.

Being an older brother carries similar responsibilities to a father, only on a miniature scale. As a brother, you can learn early on to keep a watchful eye out for baby, making sure everything is safe, in order and not a threat. As time passes, however, your new brother or sister will become more of a companion and it will be important to teach him or her how to play, share and be careful around your home and outdoors.

You will be asked to watch out for baby so that nothing dangerous happens. You have a big responsibility, if you want it, and you know your parents will be so appreciative of what you do to help them.

ANGELIC GUIDANCE

Now that I have a younger sibling, I need help in developing a sense of responsibility and maturity and to become capable of responding to the needs of my new baby brother or sister. Please help me to keep a careful eye out for baby and help my parents when they ask something of me. Help me to understand and know I am loved also and that baby is an addition to my life, not a threat.

Angelic Prayer

Dearest Angel of Brothers, help me to see the gifts of being a big brother to this new baby. Help me be kind, loving and attentive. I know that I can be caring and responsible if I try. I want baby to be a friend and to look up to me with affection and pride all our lives. I want to be a good big brother and help my sibling feel safe in life and be happy.

 ## Meditation

Being an older brother requires that I pay attention to my new sister or brother. I can help mother by doing what she asks of me and support my father by sharing and playing with him when he needs a companion. I can see that baby rests quietly, and is not threatened in any way when alone. I know I am equally as important to my parents as the new baby. Babies simply need a lot of attention in the beginning of their lives, just like I once did. I will try to accept that truth and be comfortable with it now.

93

Grandmothers

"I offer my love and nurturing to this baby throughout my life. I share my pride, joy and love with my children and grandchildren; they are blessings in my life"

There is nothing sweeter in life than the love a grandmother has for her grandchildren. A grandmother is relieved of the burden of parenting, with its constant vigilance and chores, yet you can delight in each new baby. You can choose when and how much to participate in the baby's life and you can share your pride in this new baby with all your family and friends. Being a grandmother is worthy of constant celebration.

You can enjoy the wonder of being a loving grandmother and experience that special bond that a grandmother's love creates in her grandchildren's lives. You have the opportunity to be a guardian and guide, and to open doors to the world for your grandchild.

As a grandmother, you can pass on a lifetime's wisdom, humour and truth by setting an example of happiness, health, wellbeing and joy. You can be a fairy godmother in disguise and make everything all right for this new child and his or her family. Grandmothers help the angels do their jobs.

Angelic Prayer

*Dearest Angel of Grandmothers, thank you
for the blessing of my being able to see my
child step into the role of parent. I ask that the
depth of my wisdom and the truth of my love
find their way into the heart of my
grandchild. I know that the strengths and joys
of my life are part of this baby's heritage and
will influence his or her life in hidden and
mysterious ways. Help me be a loving
grandmother, full of love and grateful for the
opportunity to help.*

 ## Meditation

*I thank my good fortune in being able to
experience the wonders of being a
grandmother. I know that my role is one of
guide, friend and support for my children
as they raise their baby. I do not want to
interfere but I do want them to know I love
and care for them. Let me reflect on what
ways I can be of help, and how I can
participate joyfully in family life.*

95

Grandfathers

"I provide wise guidance and the depth of my life experience to help my grandchild find his or her way in the world. I am proud and honoured to be a grandfather"

ANGELIC GUIDANCE

I seek help in participating in the life of my new grandchild. I have so much to offer that could help a young child find his or her way to truth, remain healthy and discover wonderful and exciting things. Help me feel I have something worthwhile to contribute to the lives of my progeny. Enable me to feel comfortable and safe in myself so I can respect the boundaries of this little child and be appropriate in my behaviour with him or her. I want to offer real wisdom and truth to a new generation.

Blessed are the grandfathers who delight in the birth of their grandchildren. As a grandfather, you have a small and passive role to play at the beginning of a grandchild's life but eventually, with time, you can be a guide and source of knowledge, wisdom and even adventure.

Taking a grandchild fishing, teaching him or her to build things the old-fashioned way, or telling stories that leave an indelible mark on a child's soul because they are stories that carry a moral impulse – these are all things you as a grandfather can do; you have the capacity to communicate practical advice and be the bearer of truth and spiritual wisdom.

Blessed are the men who respond to young children with knowledge and wisdom. It doesn't take much to include a child in a conversation, listen to what his or her hopes and dreams are, or find out what delights and what frightens. Being a grandfather offers an opportunity to show tenderness, kindness and concern for a small person trying to find the moral guideposts of life.

Angelic Prayer

Dearest Angel of Grandfathers, I ask your blessing as I take on the role of grandfather. Help me to be a teacher, guide and protector of this new generation and allow me to offer healing for the young. I can help a child accept his or her vulnerability and come to terms with any limitations. I want to provide unconditional love for this young soul and help him or her feel cherished and accepted.

 ## Meditation

I know that I can be a wonderful grandfather. As I reflect on ways I can support my grandchild coming into life, I see that by setting an example of integrity and kindness I can create a powerful influence on this child. I can spend time with my grandchild and teach him or her things that may help in life. I have a capacity for patience and acceptance that the parents may be too busy to possess. For example, I can sit for a long time sharing stories or demonstrating simple tasks that will make a young child's mind creative and productive. It is a real blessing to share what I know about life with this child.

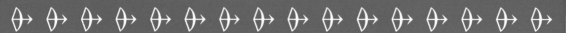

SAGITTARIUS BABIES

Sagittarians are brave, optimistic, confident, curious and seek adventure with a probing intelligence. They basically have few fears, love speed, and can disregard the rules of conventional behaviour and attract danger. They have a tendency to question authority so you'll need to keep a watchful eye on your child and set boundaries. It's best to be clear and honourable when you set the rules so you don't find your authority challenged.

Sagittarians love sports and the outdoors and to travel and find new adventures for their restless natures. Your child's love of adventure will have her strike out on her own early in life.

They want to see people happy and your child will try to cheer you up if you are down. Sagittarians are extravert by nature, intelligent, happy and fun-loving. They are, at heart, loveable, likeable and intelligent idealists. One of their great strengths is they do believe that tomorrow will be better than today.

They have open and cheerful natures that invite friendship and an exchange of ideas. They make and are wonderful friends. They have clever minds and are good students They love nature, especially animals, and often espouse causes aimed at the underdog. They can be counted on to participate in making their world a better place for the less fortunate. They are generous with their time and efforts.

Strong, athletic and sturdy, they can be a bit awkward at times and are prone to tripping or falling easily. When they take ill, they have very strong recuperative powers. They do not linger in a sick bed and are soon on their feet and out the door again, seeking more adventures.

ANGELIC GUIDANCE

Help me to guide this curious and intelligent child carefully so that all her gifts persist and her shortcomings do not interfere with her destiny. Help my child discover the beauty and wonder of life in all its various forms. Let my dear one always be safe, away from harm's way and protected by your loving wings. Help my child control her temper and find a way to express her capacity to do good, transform and heal the world around her.

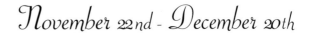

November 22nd - December 20th

A Sagittarian's negative side is that her temper flares easily and she will not back down from a fight or resist conflict. Sagittarius children are free of malice but they can have tempers and often blurt out strong and shocking statements in total innocence. They always mean well, however, even if they are not understood, as they are somewhat naïve.

Be prepared for a very curious child – investigating, challenging and seeking truth. If you are fair in creating a safety system to protect your child, she will respect your values. If you create a system that is too tight, you can count on being challenged. Your child can detect dishonesty and pretense and will question the rules. As a parent, offer your child wisdom and love for the truth and help her cultivate a sense of economy in all she does.

Dearest Angel of Sagittarius Babies, I pray for my child always to be safe and, at the same time, always free to explore the natural and spiritual worlds so she experiences the wonder of life. Help me inculcate fairness, honesty and love in her heart. I pray that my baby rejoices in the love we provide at home and grows to honour the family, respecting her parents and her roots.

Aunts

"I support my family in looking after this new baby, helping where I can and being an important part of this child's life"

Blessed are the women who take on the role of aunt to a new baby. You offer the best of your knowledge and wisdom to help a young mother cope with the challenges of parenting. Although you, as an aunt, may not share the same level of intimacy as a grandmother, you may be more generationally matched to the mother and can offer the possibility of companionship to both baby and mother. You can babysit, take care of the odd chore that needs doing around the house and support a new mother in a variety of other practical ways.

As this new baby grows, you can offer your own home for fun, companionship and friendship. Whether you are a blood relative or an "honourary" aunt chosen through friendship, you can provide a lifetime of support to baby especially in each initiation baby goes through in his or her development.

Aunties make good friends, life-long companions and cherished champions when a child needs an ally or someone to be on his or her side. The angels bless the women who take on this role in happiness and joy, those women who love to share the best of themselves.

ANGELIC GUIDANCE

Help me participate in this new baby's life as a guide, companion or surrogate mother when this child's mother has to be some place other than with her child. I know that you will guide me to speak up when necessary and share my love as best I can with this new baby. I ask for the guidance to know appropriate boundaries with this family and when I can open my arms and share my love fully.

Angelic Prayer

Dearest Angel of Aunts, thank you for the deep friendship that I feel for my sister. Whether she is blood, related by marriage or simply a good friend, I cherish the role of support being offered to me. Help me share love, friendship, constancy and delightful adventures with my niece or nephew and in ways that help all the family. I want them to know they can count on me. We walk this path of parenting together. I will share in the highs and the lows that life brings. We are bonded in love that unites our families.

 ## Meditation

As I reflect on the role of aunt I seen there are opportunities to be of service. I want to be aware of when I am needed to help out with sitting, caring for baby or being a friend to my sister. Help me be a valued and cherished part of this child's life for years to come. I know that I want to celebrate birthdays, honour occasions and be there when needed.

Uncles

*"I offer my guidance
and enthusiasm in
helping this child find
his way in the world"*

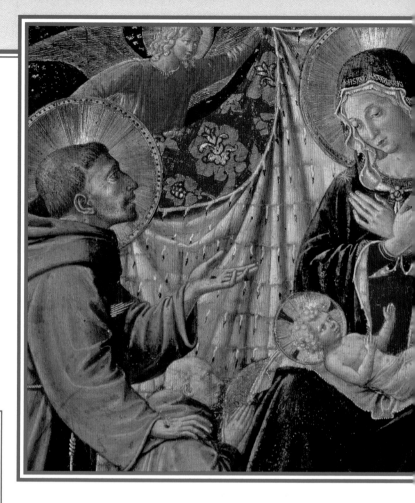

Being an uncle gives you opportunities to share your wisdom and
knowledge along with concern for your niece of nephew. You can
support your family by showing an interest in this new child and
can help when you see the new parents overwhelmed with
responsibilities. You may wish to reflect on how you can
participate in your niece's or nephew's healthly development.

Being an uncle allows you to share in the joys of extended
family life. You have the possibility of allowing love and respect

Angelic Prayer
• • • • • • • • • • • • • • •

Dearest Angel of Uncles, I rejoice in the relationship I have with this new baby. Help me be protective and influential in helping baby mould a wholesome and healthy world view. Help me be a strong and loving presence in this child's life and for his or her parents to know they can count on me when they need help.

Meditation

I choose to participate in this child's life as a loving and caring uncle. I would like to be close, caring and available for my niece or nephew and enjoy her or his company often. I know I have a great capacity to love children and to share their experiences. I can teach, guide and support as a blessed uncle.

into your life from the children of your siblings. You can exhibit your love by sharing in the care and education of this baby over the years of his or her growth and maturity.

Your nephew or niece inevitably will be curious about how you and his or her parents grew up and experienced life. You are a repository of family memories and can add a different perspective to this child's world view. Enjoy the role of being an uncle. It is a blessing to guide and protect new life.

Godparents

"I honour the responsibility of being a spiritual guardian for this child. I accept the task and respect the duty"

Godparents are designated as spiritual protectors for a new baby. This is a role taken very seriously and honoured both in the church and by the family as a solemn responsibility that is meant to last a lifetime.

A godparent brings levity and forethought to the task of guiding a child through the passages and initiations of life. It is a role that has ancient ties whereby aunts, uncles or close family friends take on the responsibility of protecting a child should the parents be compromised or die. People have always taken this role seriously.

Godparents provide a reminder that spiritual development is important and crucial for the wholesome growth of a child. It entails much more than sending a birthday card or holiday gift. A true godparent knows what is happening in the daily life of his or her godchild and sees where he or she can add value to that child's life. A godparent supports healthy change, has a say in the decisions that affect a child's life and is there should anything happen in the family where he or she can be of help.

Angels stand behind godparents and help them bring deliberation, healing and due consideration to any discussion about the welfare of their godchildren. Angels know to listen to the prayers of godparents when they pray for their godchildren. They also help each child know he or she will be protected and guided on this earthly plane.

ANGELIC GUIDANCE

As a godparent you have the responsibility of a young soul in your care. You look after his or her spiritual welfare and, in some cases, physical welfare if anything should happen to his or her family. It is a serious task and asks you to be willing to be available when called upon. You can seek angelic guidance through prayer and meditation if you have problems making a decision for your godchild. You know that each time you offer up a prayer for this child's benefit, your prayer will be carried to the heavenly realm and your petition lovingly considered.

Angelic Prayer

Beloved Angel of Godparents, thank you for the honour of having been chosen to look after this child's spiritual and physical welfare. I take this task seriously and promise to honour what is asked of me throughout my life. I will take care to consider what is best for my godchild and I ask your help in making good and wholesome decisions that best serve this child's destiny and heartfelt interest.

 ## Meditation

As you consider what is asked of you as a godparent reflect back on your own life and those people who acted as godparents or responsible guardians for your welfare. How did they guide you towards being a spiritual being, a fulfilled person and a responsible adult? You may wish to consider that much is being asked of you now as you step into the role of spiritual guide to this young child.

CAPRICORN BABIES

A Capricorn baby is calm and deliberate in his actions. If you place a toy before him, just out of his reach, he will attempt to retrieve it and you may be surprised how easily he accomplishes this task without feeling thwarted or frustrated. His is a serious little soul with a great tenacity for life.

ANGELIC GUIDANCE

I need to ensure that my baby finds warmth and love with his family and friends. Show me ways I can encourage my baby to feel he belongs, is a part of a family and community and is loved by all. I wish to temper any sense of separation that sets my baby apart. I know that he has his life and I wish to add warmth, love and joy to the crucible that helps create his life. Give me the strength to match my baby's strong will and to help be a guiding force. Show me how to help my baby gain confidence in his abilities and to ease his way in life so there are minimal disappointments.

Capricorns, like the goat to whom they are connected, are very sure footed and have strong feet. They also have capable hands and love making practical things. They may appear harmless but are, by nature, very tough. They will hammer away persistently towards their goals. They can endure hardship, insults and cruel disappointments calmly. Even as children you will see in them an ability to achieve their goals. They learn to cope with duty and responsibility and can manage frustration better than most signs.

They are known to steadily follow the upward path and have great respect for authority and tradition. As children, they are very good students – focused, disciplined and accountable. As adults, they have good business heads and earthy ambitions. They court success. They seldom stumble and you may see your Capricorn baby walk at an early age and not look back.

Capricorns have sober, solitary natures and will have a few good friends. They can appear melancholic and are weaker than most babies but quickly develop strength and resiliency and have a great capacity for survival and endurance. They can be pessimistic and full of fear and uncertainty, and this is where positive parenting skills can help them overcome their worries. As a

December 21st - January 19th

parent you want to encourage your child to be confident and to venture outdoors

A Capricorn matures early and is capable of communicating his needs without tantrums. Your child will be definite about getting his message across and will wait to see your response. He will be patient and bide his time to get what he wants. A Capricorn child can wear you down in the end.

Your baby will do well with when there is routine and rhythm in his life. He will love order and will even keep his toys in a specific place and be upset when you move them.

. . . .

Dearest Angel of Capricorn Babies, *I pray that my baby can grow into a loving, responsible adult, who is capable of warmth, trust and kindness. Help soften his hard edges; give him inner warmth to sustain him in times of trial and hardship. I would like to offer my love to support this tender and dear soul as he grows and matures into a person of compassion and love, as well as being a capable leader.*

ANGELS AND BABIES

However your baby arrives on this earth – boy or girl, singly or with one or more siblings, premature, ill or with developmental delay – or sadly, with limited time to live, there are angels who will look after him or her. Of course, the angels are there to thank when you have a safe and healthy delivery but it is particularly important to reach out to them when you are confronted with a difficult or challenging situation such as illness, disability or death.

If you didn't have a spiritual context before, this might be a time to consider developing one. It is very difficult to see a baby suffer, or go through the challenges of developmental delay, without a spiritual understanding. And this is even more important if your baby dies. Nothing is more painful than the loss of a child. An ocean of grief is created that appears limitless and which takes great strength and courage to climb out of. If you are able to hold loss within the context of your spiritual beliefs, you have an advantage over someone who does not share your emotional capabilities.

As a parent of a child with special needs or one who has died, you are blessed with the love of angels. They will provide you with the spiritual sustenance you need to get through the hard times and, eventually, find a peace that allows you to carry on with your life.

Angels bless us all the time and, as painful as the challenges seem, you are meant to overcome them and find a better way forward.

PART

8

In Raphael's painting of the Madonna of the Blue Diadem, *Mary has lifted a protective veil from her sleeping baby while keeping a protective hand around the young St. John the Baptist, the Christ child's cousin. Mary gazes tenderly at her infant son – like any mother with a newborn. Blue is a colour often associated with Mary and symbolises heavenly grace.*

Baby Girls

"I love my little girl.
I accept her feminine spirit
has a place of honour
in my heart"

ANGELIC GUIDANCE

I ask for guidance in helping me be a strong and independent-thinking parent so that I raise my daughter to become her own woman. I want to be able to show my child the options that are available to her so that her destiny can unfold. Help her know who she is and what she wants in life. If she chooses a career, help her find the willpower to withstand the challenges and trials that come with that choice. Whatever she wants to do or be in life, help her find her way to the halls of opportunity. Let her be guided and influenced by good people who understand the spiritual aspects of life and who are not just interested in the material world.

It is an honour to bring a baby girl into the world. The sweetness and tenderness of a baby girl can simply melt a hardened heart and open a channel for deep healing to transpire. A girl born into the world today carries the promise and hope for a better, more enlightened tomorrow as well as the prospects for future generations. Girls not only have the possibilities of expressing their intelligence and developing mastery in almost any field of endeavour, they also are able to bring new life into the world. If you have given birth to a baby girl rejoice that this is a time in history when your baby can become anything she wishes. She has entry into educational institutes and government, the corporate world or the sciences. There is nothing she cannot achieve if she sets her mind to it.

A baby girl can achieve in a man's world and, at the same time, be soft, yielding and loving as a lover, partner or wife. These options are all open to her and, with your help, she will know her path in life.

Angel of Baby Girls, bless this beautiful baby and let her grow to her full capacity as a woman. Allow her to overcome obstacles, meet all challenges and find her strength and value in the world. Show her that she can develop strength of character and a good moral impulse to do good and help others. Let her understand that, as a child of the universe, her path is waiting to unfold. Protect her from all harm, give her insight into her true nature and see that she becomes the best person she can be. She is a gift to the world.

Angelic Prayer

Dearest Angel of Baby Girls, I pray that my daughter can be happy, express her true nature in a safe and meaningful manner and make a contribution to the wellbeing and healing of the world in which she lives. I ask you to help her find her way to those good people who will transform her desires into reality. I know that as her parent I seek to develop her quality of character and an internal sense of who she is and that she is capable of achieving anything she sets her heart on.

 ## Meditation

Reflect on your childhood and the dreams you had as a child. Did you want to be a teacher or doctor, an artist or scientist? What were the aspirations you shared with your family? Did you experience limitations that stood in your way from fulfilling these dreams? Are you going to allow your daughter to be limited in achieving her goals because someone says she can't or shouldn't do what she wants? How can you support her in achieving her dreams and knowing she can do what she wants with her life? Write down the answers you receive from Spirit so that one day your daughter can know you opened a channel for her life to unfold in an easy and effortless way through your thoughts and reflections. She will honour you for this.

Baby Boys

*"I love my son.
He is my pride and joy"*

The qualities of manhood that your baby boy will espouse are those that have pervaded the male world for millenia. The changes that are now on the horizon offer him the opportunity of developing an emotional and spiritual aspect of himself that is new and unheard of in human history till recently.

Previously, boys grew into manhood through a series of initiations that toughened them up, made them courageous and fearless and gave them outer strength. Today, as we have evolved into a more spiritual dimension, we are beginning to value the inner core values that define a man such as the strength of integrity, the ability to express and share emotions with others and to cultivate a sense of inner worth that allows him to be soft, caring and spiritual. This is new.

In truth, men are starting to change roles with the opposite sex. Females, who were traditionally bound to the inner realms and excluded from achieving external power are now "out there" in the world. Males, who had previously cultivated external prowess are now transforming their hardened exteriors into more malleable interiors, which allow them to feel emotion and seek a higher spiritual plane.

This evolution has been long in coming. Not only is it re-defining the sexes, it is transforming the world in which babies come into life. Now there are no longer rigid expectations about the roles gender defines. The angels have no preferences and love boys and girls alike. They offer sensitivity to young men to see their inner nature and strength and courage to young girls so they can over come fear and limitations.

ANGELIC GUIDANCE

I ask for help for my young boy as he opens up to the world of discovery and adventure. This world, once so defined as the material, physical world around us, is now a vast inner realm of subtleties, which cover a new canvas of expression. Help my child know who he is, what he wants and how, with proper guidance, he can achieve what his heart desires.

Angelic Prayer

Dearest Angel of Baby Boys, help my son know his worth and discover the depths of his spirit as well as find his talents and gifts that will take him into the world. Help him develop strength of character as well as physical strength, tenderness and vulnerability. Enable him to think clearly and logically, and to express his feelings in a loving and caring way to whomever comes to share his life.

Meditation

The world has been ruled for thousands of years by the male mind. It is changing now to a more equal status for men and women. I want my son to be able to adapt to this truth and not insult or disparage the women in his life. He will be very unhappy if he cannot accept the females in his life as his equals, his teachers and his partners. I can help him adapt to this change by setting an example for him to see. I will not allow the women in his life (and mine) to be put down and diminished; I will not let him grow up thinking that is acceptable. I will encourage all women to stand up for themselves in pride so he will know what a strong independent woman is and want one in his life. My partner and I can create a crucible for our son to develop wholesome attitudes about life, the opposite sex and his place in the world. We will affirm one another and let our son know he can do what he wants and be happy.

113

Twins and Multiples

*"Each child is unique
and worthy of
individual expression"*

Twins and multiple siblings are fascinating. Although they share the same womb for nine months, they can be very different – even if they appear identical. When each baby is considered an individual with her own rights to life and own particular forms of self expression, each will thrive.

Babies who come in pairs or multiples can lose their individual sense of self too easily. Their mothers may be too busy with daily care to consider each child separately and to express their love appropriately. When each experiences her individual self and is encouraged to cultivate her own wants and desires, parents may have more work during childhood but will be proud of the efforts each child is making on her own behalf.

Babies, no matter how they come, are separate souls. They share a kinship with any sisters or brothers, but they are unique and demand to be experienced as such. Rivalry may be a way in which this individuality is expressed or alternatively, an unnatural closeness can occur, which may be difficult to deal with.

Parents can work together to support the efforts of each child to be her own person. When you study each of your children carefully, you will see what is unusual and unique to her. There will be certain defining characteristics that will show up early in life that will be distinguishing marks for a child's entire life. Take the time to understand each child and to know her hopes, fears, desires and personal markers.

Angels help us develop a grace and consciousness as part of our evolutionary path. They support our healing from past wounds, and our belief in ourselves as people capable of meeting our destiny. They know we are here to bring healing to the world. Twins and multiple births are ways of bringing that grace and consciousness in quantity.

ANGELIC GUIDANCE

Help me help each one of my babies express his or her own identity clearly and in a style that we can come to know who is that son or daughter. Help me to create a bond of love between my children and, at the same time, help them form their own individual lives. If there is a place where one can help or support the other, let that become evident. Help my babies to know they are each loved for whom he or she is.

Angelic Prayer

Dearest Angel of Twins and Multiple Births, thank you for the gift of these babies. They are double the love, double the fun and double the challenge to raise. Show us how we can be good parents, appropriate guides and teachers so the babies can cultivate strong, individual personalities and be capable of their own choices, with enough will to move into life in a positive way.

Meditation

Be aware that each child has her own talents, gifts and personality. These babies are not alike except in appearance; each has her own destiny to fulfill in life. How you help your babies realise who each one is depends on your ability to see each child for whom she is. Can you spend time alone with each child as your babies are growing up and get to know who lives in each body? Are you willing to support each child in expressing her wishes, desires and hopes so that each feels she can make a happy and responsible life? This is as much your choice to see your babies as individuals as it is for them to bring their personalities forward to be seen.

115

AQUARIUS BABIES

Babies born in Aquarius come from the spirit realm to help build and create a better future for humanity. They have unique qualities that convey an expanded outlook with little or no prejudice. They have a profound sense of brotherhood, love people and have many friends throughout their lives.

Angels of Aquarius babies have their work cut out for them, however. These children are often unpredictable, have their heads in the clouds daydreaming of the future and can be accident prone. They need love, strong guidance to stay present and focused and prayers to their guardian angels to watch out and protect them.

ANGELIC GUIDANCE

I ask you for help in creating rhythm and order so that my baby can develop healthy life habits that bring out the best in him. What things should I change to create a sense of discipline, order and harmony in my home?

Aquarians can be full of surprises. Though they are not naturally trusting, they always seek the truth. They are true idealists who early in life formulate their own codes, which colour their outlook on life. Although many child prodigies are Aquarians, the majority mature late in life.

It is said of Aquarius children that you will chase them into the future. They are sensitive, stubborn, independent, evasive and impulsive. Their great strength is the lightening speed with which their minds work. They are quick to grasp the true nature of people and situations and despise lies and cheating.

They can be commanding. They appear calm and docile to the eye but are unpredictable and full of contrary actions and thoughts. It is not an easy thing to parent an Aquarian child, and it is best not to try to figure one out. He requires his parents to step back and permit him to make his own decisions. You can help by setting good boundaries and encouraging your child to act on his decisions and to follow through on these pursuits.

Aquarians are so alert that their nervous systems often are fragile. They require ample sleep, good nutrition and exercise. They can tend towards laziness and may need to be taught at an early age

January 20th – February 18th

to enjoy the outdoors and routine exercise. Because they are so sensitive they can be easily disturbed by unspoken tensions in the home; they do see into the soul and are capable of hearing what is unspoken.

You should encourage your Aquarian child to find tranquillity and harmony and develop concentration and memory. His physical weakness is his circulatory system – all the more reason to encourage exercise and outdoor activity. You also want to avoid harsh words that can create exaggerated fears.

* *

Dearest Angel of Aquarius Babies, please watch over and protect my child from harm. Help keep his attention on the tasks at hand and help me instill discipline and order into our daily life so that my child can develop the habits that will best support grounding his ideas in reality. I ask for patience and a wholesome attitude to parenting such a wondrous child into adulthood.

Premature Babies

"My baby thrives, grows and finds her way safely into life"

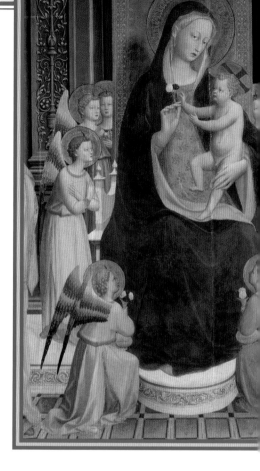

Babies born before their due date are generally very quick, full of the life force and eager to be alive. When you see them you may be amazed at how much energy they have. They are little dynamos.

These babies have come " early" because they just wanted to be in the world so much. They exhibit an unusual enthusiasm, which babies who have gestated longer in the womb do not have. Sometimes, they struggle for air and their breathing can be laboured so they need to be monitored and watched vigilantly. Helping them relax into themselves is the work of parents and caregivers. The more these babies can relax and feel safe, the easier it is for them to thrive.

Babies choose the times and places of their births. They have their own internal clocks and for whatever reason, they know when they must come forth into the world. We need to honour their timing and see that their needs are completely met. That

ANGELIC GUIDANCE

I ask the angels to help me tune my internal clock to that of my baby's in order to become aligned to her needs. I need to find the grounded, constant rhythms that will support us in waking together, eating at about the same time and being similarly active. I ask that my angel and my baby's angel work at creating unity so that when it is time for a rest, we can nap together, for example. I ask the angels to help me create the space in my day in which I can keep my baby close to my body, so she can hear my heartbeat and know I am there for love, care and protection – just as the angels are there.

means we have to give them a sense of safety, provide the nourishment they crave and keep them warm, safe and comfortable while their delicate nervous systems adapt to life outside the womb.

When given optimal conditions premature babies can grow quickly. They can take nourishment, put on weight and "catch up" to their growth curve. They are eager babies and knowing this about them helps you to understand their quick tempers, their easy irritability and their unusual curiosity about life.

If your baby is premature, you can support her in every step of her growth and development by recognising her predisposition to quick, rapid development and her need for security and safety. She has an active internal clock that tells her she is hungry, tired or in need of care. When you pay attention to her requests for feeding, changing or sleeping, you honour her and aid her development.

Tune into the Angel of Premature Babies and ask how you can help your child come into the world in a safe way. It can direct your attention to an even and consistent pace of life that avoids chaos and rapid change; your rhythmic flow throughout your day needs to be attuned to your baby and you need to be extra vigilant to help her when she is in distress.

Angelic Prayer

Beloved Angel of Premature Babies, please guide me towards establishing a healthy and wholesome rhythm in our lives that will keep my baby happy, nourished and comfortable while she adapts to life. I ask you to keep me alert to changes that may occur with my baby that will need my focus and attention. Help me to understand what it is that I must do to help baby in every way until we are sure that she is in life and thriving. Bless this baby's courage and tenacity for wanting to be with us so much.

Meditation

When you reflect on being pregnant with your baby you may have had a sense that labour would come sooner than expected. You may have had an inkling that your baby's rhythm was faster than yours. As you care for your baby, try to establish a slower pace for your both, and a more rhythmic sense of the day and night. This means that during the day there is activity and at night there is less stimulation and you are able to have a good, full rest. When your baby is fussy and wants feeding, changing or even play time, allow yourself to take care of her needs then find your way back to rest. Keeping your baby close to you so she can hear your heartbeat and feel your body's warmth will help her adapt to your daily cycles. Be consistent, stay centred and be very patient while your little one adapts to life.

Sick Babies

"Beloved Angels, please hear my prayer that my baby is restored to health"

ANGELIC GUIDANCE

I ask you that you guide me in the right direction where I can get good help for my baby. Help me find excellent health care at the hands of reliable and compassionate professionals. If my baby can be healed with the help of an alternative method, lead me to the person who can help. If baby requires heroic intervention in an emergency room or with a medical expert, put us in good hands. Help me stay with my baby for as long as possible. I can talk to her, soothe her distress, comfort her. Help us please.

For parents it is extremely difficult to experience the helplessness of a small baby when she is ill. It wrenches the heart and upsets every one beyond reason. Knowing when to seek professional help and what kind of help is important. If your baby was born with or develops a serious health condition, you will already be in the hands of medical experts. If, however, your baby develops a minor illness such as a cold or flu, you still will be concerned and may need to reflect on making an appropriate choice as to what form of healing you will employ.

There are many emotions that may arise when a child falls ill. Guilt and shame are common while sensibility and practicality are put on hold. Your baby will be best served by the help of a rational, medically experienced advocate who can help you make wholesome choices for your child's wellbeing and health but a trusted relative or impartial friend may be able to help you find your way.

Prayer is a powerful tool for seeking spiritual help and internal guidance. Praying to the forces of love, who are part of the angelic realm and represent the Creator, is a valid way of reaching a decision. If you have turned your baby's health over to a professional, you have only one recourse and that is to pray. You pray for the good, you pray that your child recovers, you pray that you can stay strong and resilient through this challenge.

It is not an easy task to cope with a sick child. When you face this challenge remember to ask the angelic realm, particularly the Angel of Sick Babies, for help. Angels will give you the strength, support and courage to do what is necessary to bring healing. Trust your spirit to be strong and to love your baby.

Angelic Prayer

Dearest Angel of Sick Babies, help my child recover her health and restore her in every way. Help assuage my fears and give me the courage to make good decisions for my baby's care. We are in your hands. Our hopes and fears rest at your feet. Please give us a positive outcome and let all be well.

 ## Meditation

How are you going to deal with illness when it arises? This is an important question for any parent. Do you feel you can empower yourself sufficiently to learn the basics of first aid, for instance? You should, at least, have an able practitioner to assist you with treating the minor illnesses that are likely to occur. Learning how to deal with accidents or ill health often can prevent problems from taking too strong a grip. Asking for the blessing of health can create an attitude of health for you and your family. See all being well and thriving as the final outcome of your visualisation. If you have an sick baby, help her by seeing her as whole and complete in every way. Dwell on healing and not on illness. It will help your baby, too, to be held in the light of unconditional love and total acceptance. Be grateful when your baby recovers that all is well.

Babies with Developmental Delay

"I love my child unconditionally and support her in life in every way I know"

A baby that has developmental delay is still whole and complete in herself although it is easy to see such a child as imperfect or damaged. We have each been given our gifts and talents to work with, and sometimes children with developmental delay, are the best teachers to give us spiritual depth, universal connections and a fighting spirit to do the best we possibly can for them.

Many mothers of children with developmental delay tie their identities to their children. These mothers regard each challenge, defeat or victory as theirs. Sometimes, a mother needs to know that her child has her own individual destiny. When there is a healthy degree of separation, a child has an opportunity to develop at her own pace, own speed and in her own way.

Children with developmental delay can be helped in many ways. They ask your unconditional love, full support in meeting their special needs and abiding grace in helping them live optimal lives. Much has been learned about their health because there are many such children. We know, for instance, that they often thrive on special diets and therapies. Finding out what can be done to support optimal development will help you feel you are doing whatever is possible to help your child.

Developing a spiritual context that allows you to experience a challenged child as whole, complete and worthy of love, kindness and respect is also essential to her healing and to yours. God and His angels see all beings as whole and perfect in their spirit. Find the graciousness of spirit to see that love is at the core of all life. Develop your consciousness to see your child as whole, perfect and complete. From that place you can do many things to help her. Ask the angels to support all your efforts, and to hold you and your child in love, grace and beauty. They can provide you with a context of love in which healing is able to happen.

ANGELIC GUIDANCE

I ask for help in finding the right approach to healing my child. Whatever the causes of her problems, I now seek wholesome and viable solutions from doctors, therapists and healers who can take my baby forward. Help me to cultivate my own life so I am not enmeshed with my baby's life and can be objective when I need to be for her sake.

Angelic Prayer

* * * * * * * * * * * * * * * *

*Dearest Angel of Babies with Developmental Delay, Help me to find
the best resources possible for helping baby develop and grow
optimally. Help me know that baby has her own destiny and I have
mine. I know that in order for healing to happen, I need to be clear
this is my child's life path. It is not mine. I know that this awareness
is the best path I can follow to help my baby. Please open the doors
that will permit me to seek the healing that gives my baby an
opportunity for growth and development. I know that only using drugs
and medications may not lessen the delay. Help me to forgive myself
for anything I did in my past that may have created this problem. I
forgive anyone who was complicit in this problem.*

Meditation

*Dwell on the notion that if your child suffers from developmental
delay, you have many options and resources for seeking help. The
diagnosis from your doctor will give you something you can research
and understand. If you are open to alternative therapies there are
many that directly address the physical and mental problems your
child may be experiencing. Be aware that conventional medicine does
not have all the answers to these problems. You may need to seek
guidance in other arenas that will help your child mend and heal.
Stay open to possibilities, pray for guidance and cultivate a faith that
your child will be healed.*

Babies Who Die

"My baby has returned from where she came.
She rests in spirit loved forever, and was cherished during her brief time together with us"

A baby's death leaves a hole in you that is deep, raw and unbearably painful. How do you cope with this excruciating loss and this sorrow?

It gives little solace to know that your baby has returned home to the spirit realm. You are left feeling hopeless and despairing that your life will ever be filled with joy. It is a great tragedy to lose a baby and you must honour her life by feeling the grief that her parting has created in you.

Once you have allowed your time of sorrow to pass, you must move forward into life again. You may decide to have another child or adopt or foster a baby. No other child will fill the place of the one you have lost, but you must move forward into life again and find a realistic solution to what you want for yourself and your partner.

Honour the past and create a space for this baby. You may want to keep a photo of her or some other momento of the time you had together.

ANGELIC GUIDANCE

I need help in accepting this terrible loss. Help me to realise that my baby had her own destiny that did not include a long life on earth. I will always cherish the memory of this beautiful being who graced my life and touched it so fully. I grieve that she is gone. Help my partner and I find our way back into life. If we decide to have another child or take in a child in need of a home, please allow that to unfold effortlessly. Help us always to remember the beautiful being who came to us with love and so much tenderness.

Dearest Angel of Babies Who Die, I pray for the soul of my beloved child and I share my gratitude for having known her, even briefly. I have experienced the greatest love and the most unbearable loss through this child coming into my life. I would not exchange this for anything except having my baby back in my arms. Bless us that we may renew our lives; bless baby for having come to us.

 ## Meditation

Take a moment to reflect on the sorrow that has enveloped your life with the loss of your baby. What are the good moments that you remember? How would you care to cherish the memory of your baby? Can you pray for healing for your spirit, which has just undergone a horrific ordeal? Can you allow your good to come to you now as you start to step back into life? These are questions only you can answer when you are ready to release and let go of your sorrow. Bear in mind that your baby is watching over you, loving and blessing you and would want you to find renewed joy in another child.

It is only fitting that you honour this experience, weep your tears, feel your grief and then let time heal you and all those who knew and loved your baby.

PISCES BABIES

The angels of Pisces know their guidance is heard and their love acknowledged in the deeply spiritual Pisces child. Pisces is the last of the zodiacal year and embodies all the characteristics and wisdom of all the other signs.

> ### ANGELIC GUIDANCE
> I seek to value the subtle and refined aspects of life – beauty and the arts, for example – that my Pisces baby likes and thrives on. Help me to show her the beauty that surrounds her in nature, relationships and objects. I need guidance in what things I can do to promote her physical and emotional development. I've heard that Pisces like their feet massaged and need appropriate physical activity to develop strong muscles. To help dispel fears, will being held, cuddled and possibly sung to work? I believe my baby has a capacity to love music. Help me to let my baby know how much I love her and that I will stand by her always.

Those born under this sign bring a knowing from the vast realm of possibilities that helps them accommodate to life easily and effortlessly. They have strong spirits and are capable of warmth, love and understanding far beyond their years. They are always very loyal. Pisceans love to be in harmony with their surroundings and their world is a gentle one where everyone is beautiful and all actions are lovely.

Pisces is compassionate – always willing to help where there is suffering and ignorance – and non-judgmental. She never casts aspersions on those who have fallen from grace through earthly pleasures or errors of judgement of a weak character.

The strongest of all Piscean qualities is her underlying spiritual nature. She is intuitive and guided by her emotions. She experiences presentiments and, as an adult, will easily grasp the metaphysical nature of life. Pisces is said to be the fish that swims in the deep waters of life.

Pisces has difficulty staying in one place for any length of time and likes to go with the flow. This means she has a great enthusiasm for life in all its possibilities. She likes to move, experience freedom and enjoy "swimming uphill" to meet the challenges of her destiny. In your love for

February 19th - March 20th

your Pisces baby, do not be overly confining or limit her ability to explore the world. Your baby is a natural explorer and will not like being limited.

Pisceans love subtlety and will react strongly if their environments are overly bright, harsh and glaring. Music, is important to them and your baby will appreciate being sung to or having soft music around her. Pisceans love to be touched, held and rocked. You can share your love with your Pisces baby and she will soak it up with acceptance and trust.

Pisceans are very creative in seeking solutions to problems and are often not bothered by irritants that affect others. These are not troublesome children; a mother of a Pisces baby will be the first to tell you what a good child her baby is.

Being a water sign, Pisceans are emotional, deep and grasp life's true meaning. They also love the physical aspects of water so bath time, swimming and being rocked are truly pleasurable to them.

Although Pisceans can appear weak as babies, they grow into their strength as they mature. They can be shy and can avoid competition unless really encouraged to do their best. They love the stage and many become actors but because they are good with the sufferings of the world, they also make wonderful doctors and healers.

Beloved Angel of Pisces Babies, watch over our baby so that she can cultivate the inner strength and intelligence innate to her. Help this baby to make wholesome decisions and to chose what will help unfold her destiny. Allow us to understand the sensitivity this child brings into the world.

127

ACKNOWLEDGEMENTS

The author would like to offer thanks, love and gratitude to:

Bill and Rosy Edmunston, blessing us in spirit, and their daughter Betsy Evans Banks and her husband, Brian Banks, both first-rate artists and blessed friends. This book is written, with gratitude and love, from their home, Ledge Lodge, on Walker Pond, in Blue Hill, Maine.

My adopted daughter, Inelia Benz, who has gifted me with her beautiful, expanded consciousness and loving friendship.

Those dear friends, Mary Jane and HMS Crich, who offer me a place in their hearts with love, consciousness and a good laugh.

My sister, Nita Steinberg, who I have known all her life and who is now a treasured friend.

Deborah Admiral and Nina Norell for their gifts of loving consciousness. I am grateful to your both for the steady stream of support and healing that makes a book like this possible.

Amy Carroll, who saw the possibility of creating a book where babies and angels could share their blessings with the world.